My Life's Journey With Bipolar Disorder

by
Joann M. Stuhr

Strategic Book Publishing and Rights Co.

The Definitions and References section of this book includes text from the following publications and is used by the author with written permission:

Talbot, Hales, and Yudofsky; The American Psychiatric Press. *Textbook of Psychiatry,* American Psychiatric Press, Inc.; 1988; pp. 412-413, "DSM-HI-R CRITERIA FOR MANIC EPISODE."

Copyright © 1987 American Psychiatric Association. Used with permission.

Copyright © 2011

All rights reserved—Joann M. Stuhr

No part of this book may be reproduced or transmitted in any form or by any means, graphic, electronic, or mechanical, including photocopying, recording, taping, or by any information storage retrieval system, without the permission, in writing, from the publisher.

Strategic Book Publishing and Rights Co.
12620 FM 1960, Suite A4-507
Houston, TX 77065
www.sbpra.com

ISBN: 978-1-61204-207-7

Design: Dedicated Book Services, Inc. (www.netdbs.com)

Contents

Introduction v
Chapter 1: The Homestead. 1
Chapter 2: Life on the Farm. 6
Chapter 3: Cornell College 22
Chapter 4: Teaching at Burlington High School 27
Chapter 5: Okinawa 30
Chapter 6: My Sister's Wedding. 38
Chapter 7: My Niece's Wedding 40
Chapter 8: Teaching Abroad. 41
Chapter 9: Graduate School. 61
Chapter 10: A New Career at Boeing. 67
Chapter 11: Teaching at Bettendorf High School 72
Chapter 12: Hiding My Condition. 93
Chapter 13: Publishing and Awards. 97
Chapter 14: Death of My Parents. 99
Chapter 15: Traveling Abroad 106
Chapter 16: Retirement 111
Definitions and References 118

Introduction

I was born and grew up on a farm in eastern Iowa during the 1940s and 1950s. I went to a small college close to home where I earned a degree in mathematics and a secondary school teaching license. My first teaching job right out of college was as a math teacher at a high school in southeastern Iowa. After I taught there for a little while, I realized that the time to travel and really explore the world was when I was young. I decided to seek out and ultimately accept a teaching position in Germany and, later, another one in Japan. When I returned to the States in 1966, it was time to try something different. I switched gears and landed a job in the private sector as a scientific computer programmer at the Boeing Company in Seattle, Washington.

One Monday morning in 1968, when I was thirty-one years old, I reported for work as usual with the exception of not feeling very well. My head felt like slush, and it was difficult to focus on my work. I tried to concentrate but I wasn't myself; I found it difficult to keep on task with my head in so much pain. Tuesday presented the same picture with some added dizziness. When Wednesday came along, I didn't know what to do or where to go for help with my sudden depression. My head was in far greater pain than it had ever been in before.

My health deteriorated as the week progressed. I knew I wasn't very productive at work and was concerned about my job performance, which led me into an even deeper depression. This horrible feeling preyed on me in my weakened state. I knew I needed help. Not knowing what to do, I quietly laid down on a cot in the women's lounge to rest.

My next memory was waking up in a hospital. I had absolutely no recollection as to how I got there. Much to my amazement, I felt fine when I awoke in the strange hospital bed—but something was very wrong with me. What a scare! I was used to being so independent and in control. *What is going on with me?* I wondered. More importantly, would it happen again?

Chapter 1:

The Homestead

In 1923, my father emigrated from Germany to eastern Iowa to flee the economic depression of World War I. He was only twenty-three. His uncle took him in, and so he naturally landed in the agrarian culture of the 1920s and 1930s. Working as a hired hand, my father established himself as a member of the small farming community. He met my mother around the same time, and soon a courtship began.

My mother owned a 1930 Ford Model A. She and her sister would go to the different dances in the area. Mom also asked my father to accompany them to dances, which my father did. However, he never asked my mother or her sister for a dance. This caused my mother to wonder what kind of man my father was. This all changed when one of my mother's suitors came to visit. My father noticed how much she was interested in him. Dad intervened and pursued my mother. And so it was that my parents fell in love in the rural society of the beginning of the 20th century.

My mother owned some land. After she and my father fell in love, they decided to build their homestead on that land. Even though they weren't married yet, the locals would all predict not if, but when, the happy couple would actually tie the knot. After work every day, my father and mother would trek a half-mile to continue building their dream homestead. During the spring and summer of 1935, they transformed barren land into a red brick house, a barn, and a garage (for Mom's 1930 Model A). A machine shed and a corncrib were constructed soon thereafter. They also planted and cared for trees and shrubs and began a garden and an orchard.

One day, my uncle announced that there would be a party at the developing homestead. Everyone knew this would be

the anticipated wedding. That was how it was done in those days. My parents married on September 18, 1935, at Zion Lutheran Church in Davenport, Iowa. They were both in their mid-thirties. And just as my uncle had told everyone, a shivery, or barn dance, followed after the ceremony in the haymow of the new barn.

My parents were farmers of a hundred-acre tract of land near Walcott in eastern Iowa. Since Dad was a German immigrant, he had to learn to farm in the foot/pound/second system as opposed to the metric system that he had learned in Germany. But he was never afraid to ask questions, even though he'd sometimes get ridiculed in the process.

The farm developed into fields of corn and soybeans, a pasture, and some hay land. Dad raised and sold approximately 250 hogs annually. Some years, he had twenty to twenty-five steers to sell at the stockyards in Chicago, Illinois. He and my mother also had chickens, and sometimes Muscovy ducks. A few dairy cows supplied milk for the family, too.

Three rows of Norway spruce trees were planted as a windbreak in an L-shape, north of the house and west of the barn. When that mighty north wind would blow, it was frightfully chilly but landowners knew the tricks to keep the elements at bay. My parents were no exception as they continued to craft their homestead.

Between the house and the windbreak, my parents had a huge garden and a large orchard. The fruit trees were mostly apple trees with one pear tree, one peach tree, and two apricot trees. Most interesting of these trees were the apricot trees, which towered above the windbreak. When the apricot trees were laden with fruit and harvested, not only did my parents have to balance on a long ladder to pick the apricots, but they also had to avoid the huge thorns on the trees' bark. Mom canned as many apricots as she could. The supply lasted quite a few years. My favorite dessert was a piece of devil's food cake covered with thickened apricot sauce. It was delicious! In fact, many of the flavors of the farm formed my taste for different kinds of food as I grew up.

The homestead garden was immense and of irregular shape. Potatoes were planted to harvest a year's supply for our family's use. There were two huge rectangular strawberry beds. The intense heat and high humidity associated with picking strawberries didn't seem to bother my parents and sister—but it did bother me! After forty-five minutes of picking strawberries, my light skin would turn very red and I would develop excruciating headaches. When these headaches came on, I would go back into the house to lie down. My father would say, "Joann places more strawberries in her mouth than in her box!" (Admittedly, I couldn't argue against him.) My parents sold some of the strawberries commercially. Mostly, our family liked to take the fresh strawberries and turn them into frozen strawberry jam. Breakfast was amazing when my mother made hot breakfast toast with frozen strawberry jam spread on top.

Aside from strawberries, my parents also grew broccoli, cauliflower, and large heads of cabbage. Mom planted a row of bright orange marigolds near these vegetables. The odor of the marigold blossoms was one the rabbits did not like; the flowers helped keep the rabbits away from the cabbage plants in the garden.

The tomato plants looked like little trees with the support of a cylindrical hog wire creation for the tomato branches. This way, the tomato branches were not on the ground; the tomatoes wouldn't rot. There were also rows of beets, carrots, and green beans, as well as a few radishes and green onions. Scattered around the premises were black raspberry plants, red raspberry plants, red stalks of rhubarb, currant bushes, gooseberry bushes, and grape vines. Where they weren't ripe fruits and vegetables, there were beautiful flowers: zinnias, dahlias, gladioli, columbines, asters, phlox, and begonias. Climbing roses and single roses were abundant, too. The single rose garden was east of the garage, surrounded by white sweet alyssum on the front and coral-bells and irises near the garage wall.

I grew up on this homestead. When my parents built it, they began to put down the foundation of my formative years. The homestead touched my work ethic, morals, and attitude toward my self-image. I don't know if my parents really thought about that when they turned the farm into a home, but since it was such a genuine expression of them—they interacted with it naturally—I picked that up. It never occurred to me that we could live anywhere else. To this day, that old homestead has a special spot in my heart.

Chapter 2:

Life on the Farm

When my father first saw my mother, she was in a pair of old overalls. He instantly made fun of her. At the time, he did not know that this overalls-wearing woman would become his life mate. My parents worked on their farm while raising my sister and me. I recall them holding hands in public and expressing genuine affection toward each other most of the time. As they nurtured crops, livestock, and their little family, they grew together as a strong couple, too. This was always in the background as I grew up on the farm.

When I was about one-and-a-half years old, I remember going out of the house with my father while my mother was pregnant with my sister. My mother had a difficult time with her pregnancies; she was close to forty years old when she gave birth to us. My father would take me out to the barn or put me in the wagon when it was time for him to do his chores. The farm became my world to satisfy my mind. At a very early age, I was exposed to the work, smells, sounds, and feels of the buildings, livestock, crops, and fresh and not-so-fresh air. But none of it deterred me. I felt very comfortable with the surroundings of the farm.

When I would go outside to see my dad, I shouted, "Papa-Daddy, wo bist du?" ("Daddy, where are you?") My parents were bilingual in English and Platt Deutsch (Low German). My father was insistent that his children should learn Low German before we started school, and he succeeded in that. Since I had the run of the farm, often my parents could not find me. They would shout my name to which I often responded, "Hier bin ich!" ("Here I am!") On one occasion, they found me in the corncrib, shelling kernels of corn from the cobs.

When Dad sold two hundred-pound hogs to Oscar Mayer, he would haul small loads on his pick-up truck with high sideboards. It was difficult to load them and required assistance. I sometimes helped him with the boards and gates. All of that dust, dirt, the smells, and squealing of the hogs wasn't particularly enjoyable, but it went with the territory! My parents were dedicated workers, to say the least. On top of the morning chores, Dad usually did all of the potato harvesting and picked most of the strawberries. My sister—who was two years younger than me—and I also did our fair share of the work, but it was nothing compared to what my parents managed to do on a daily basis.

"Rote Grüt," or red rice, was Dad's favorite entrée to make for our evening meal. The recipe he referred to was from Germany. Mom picked the currants when they were red and ripe and mixed them with washed red and black raspberries. This mixture was placed in a large kettle with a proper amount of water and then cooked so it could be pureed. The large amounts of juice were canned in quart bottles. When the rote grüt was prepared, several stalks of rhubarb were cooked in water in a large kettle. Next, a quart of the currant-raspberry juice was added along with more water. Cream of rice was used to thicken the mixture. Dad ate the chilled rote grüt in a soup bowl with milk poured over it. He ate this every evening meal in the hot summer, claiming that it refreshed him.

Dad had a team of workhorses, Beauty and Blue Grass, to help him in the fields. Beauty was a beautiful brown horse with a white star on her forehead. Blue Grass was a Schimmel gelding. I've seen gray horses run in the Kentucky Derby; Blue Grass's skin was a light gray with a multitude of darker spots. From a distance, Blue Grass looked like a large gray horse. My grandfather had had several teams of horses that he used to transport goods from one village to another in Germany. He had a variety of vehicles, along with a funeral hearse and a marriage carriage, too. My father and his brothers had to care for the horses, i.e., groom them, polish their harnesses, feed the horses, and clean the horse stalls. At the age of five, my dad let me hold the reins of Beauty and Blue Grass while I stood near the top of a ladder in front of the hay wagon. Hay was cut and then left in the field. The hay loader was an elevator-type device with high sideboards that dumped the loose hay into the hay wagon. The hay would then have to be forklifted to the haymow. Needless to say, I was proud that my father let me do this!

We went from the Horse Era to the One-Tractor Era to the Two-Tractor Era. I'm sure Dad found it difficult to sell his beloved horses. Dad also had a mare named Daisy. Daisy produced colts that became workhorses that Dad would then sell. Whenever Daisy was in heat, Dad would quickly phone Mr. Stallion Man. When Mr. Stallion Man and his stallion appeared on the premises, Mom would usher my sister and me to the sun porch where she would draw the shades and close the curtains entirely. She didn't want us to witness what was going on outside with Daisy and the stallion. So be it!

The time had come to train a new workhorse. With full harnesses on the three horses, Dad attached Beauty and Blue Grass to the double tree in front of the manure spreader, which was Dad's heaviest piece of equipment. Then the new workhorse was attached by a single tree in front of the manure spreader to the right side of Beauty. Dad stood within the manure spreader, holding all the reins from the horses in his left hand and a long whip in his right hand. Then, in circles, he got the horses to move around and around. Whenever the new horse bucked or kicked, Dad gave it the full crack of the whip. I was totally amazed at the physical strength of my father whenever he worked with the horses.

My mother's maternal and fraternal grandparents were born in Germany and immigrated to the United States. My mother's parents had eleven children—four of whom died young in age, with three dying of diphtheria. On her deathbed, Grandma Matilda "Tillie" Paustian asked to speak to her eldest daughter, Meta. She asked Meta to come home from Davenport, where she was working as a secretary for a lawyer, to keep the family together. At the time of their mother's death, Meta was twenty-four, Martha was ten, and Clarence was six years of age. Later, at the age of seventeen or eighteen, Martha went to work as a hired girl for Meta and her family. Fred and Meta Kronenberg's three daughters, Alice, Martha, and Leona were close to my mother. They didn't mind having Aunt Martha around.

My parents married two years before George A. Maxwell and Alice Kronenberg married. Thirteen years after that, the Maxwells moved to the Kronenberg farm that was adjacent to our farm. Maggie and Bobby Maxwell and my sister, Madeleine, and I took swimming lessons at the Natatorium in Davenport; our mothers took turns driving us there. Mom and Dad would often babysit George and Alice's four youngest children—Burdette, Maria, Edward, and Johannes—while George and Alice would go dancing and partying. My mother loved babysitting and enjoyed playing games with the children. She and Alice became very close over the years. Mom even became a confidante for Alice, but I never found out what Alice was confiding in her about because Mom never broke Alice's trust.

On Martha's birthday, the whole family went over to her house to celebrate. "Happy Birthday to you! Happy Birthday to you! Happy Birthday, dear Martha, Happy Birthday to you . . ." we sang in unison. All of my aunts and uncles and their children were there to show their support. The women and young adults played a card game called Five Hundred. Prizes were awarded for Five Hundred. The men all had piles of coins on the table and settled up once the game was over. Other games the men played included Skat and Schopfskopf. For lunch, we would all eat sandwiches and eggs on halves of buns. There were plates of sandwiches on each table. Coffee was also readily served, followed by Jell-O and cake. Aunt Luella Paustian, Clarence's wife, made the *best* white cake I have ever tasted. It was covered with boiled frosting and coconut. The celebrating didn't stop there. The next birthday party came a few days later: Dad's birthday was on June 3. Sadly, these fun and elaborate birthday parties do not exist today. They were discontinued as time went along and as families spread across the United States.

School days were also much different when I was a child compared to what children learn and experience today. Yes, my good ol' fashioned school days of reading, writing, and arithmetic were all to the tune of a hickory stick. Like the large birthday parties, that one-room country school I went to is now a thing of the past. But I still have so many memories of that place. My sister and I attended a one-room country school from kindergarten through eighth grade. Dad usually drove us to school in the morning and brought us home again when school was out, especially whenever there was inclement weather. Sometimes, we walked home from school or rode our bicycles to and from school. I remember one icy morning Dad's car did a complete 360-degree turn on sheer ice. Somehow, he managed to keep control and continued going straight ahead. That incident gave me the chills.

I began kindergarten at Fairview Number Three School, a one-room country school. The administrators kept a school log, or school history book. On the day I started school, my teacher wrote my name in the school history book with the comment: "Joann is bright." I know this because after the one-room country schools closed, and there was consolidation of schools in Iowa, the students from Fairview Number Three School held periodic reunions, enabling me to look in the school history book and read my teacher's compliment from when I was a kindergartner.

The north wall of the one-room schoolhouse had a large chalkboard for arithmetic, spelling, and writing. We were given a one-hour lunch period and two recesses—one in the morning and one in the afternoon. Each recess was fifteen minutes in length. That left four class periods each day. Some were one hour and fifteen minutes long; others were one hour and thirty minutes.

The first period was always devoted to English: reading, spelling, or writing. The second period was arithmetic. The third period was two days of health or two days to science. If we didn't have health or science during the third period, we would learn about art—usually doing something with construction paper. The fourth period was dedicated to two days of American history, two days of American government, or one day of Iowa history.

Every school day began with the Pledge of Allegiance to the United States of America. Then the focus went to the recitation bench in front of the teacher's desk; every class recited or answered questions from the teacher. Meanwhile, the students who weren't at the recitation bench had to tune out the students who were there in order to get his or her assignments finished. I'm not sure how the teacher was able to plan all of these lessons and stay organized with so much going on. The teacher also always had homework papers to correct, too. Furthermore, she had to stoke the furnace to keep us all warm in the cold months. I guess it's fair to say that she really had to "stoke" herself for the onslaught of a full day each morning! It's a marvel what these one-room school teachers accomplished.

Seventh and eighth graders had to take a State of Iowa eighth grade examination. I scored 92.7 percent in the seventh grade and 93.8 percent in the eighth grade. I was proud of my scores. At the eighth grade graduation ceremonies, I received the I Award, which was given to me and other deserving graduates by Superintendent Harry Banze for having the highest scores on the eighth grade examination in Scott County.

County spelling bees were held with the township winners from that county. I was a township winner who lost on the word, "competition," spelling out, "C-o-m-p-e-t-i-o-n." I accidentally omitted a "t" and an "i." It's ironic that this misspelled word was "competition" when, in reality, I was a good competitor!

The big production of the year was the Christmas program. All parents were invited, and the entire student body sang Christmas carols in front of them. Skits and short plays were also performed, along with an occasional comedian.

Fond memories include playing Fox and Goose in the new fallen snow during part of the lunch period and playing softball during part of the lunch period, weather permitting.

The drama bug hit me again when I was a senior in high school. I played the role of Mother Rosenbaum on Saturday night in the production, "Innocents Abroad." Her character was a gruff woman who nearly stabbed someone. Then, in "Neu Ulm," I played Catherine Petkoff in a USO production of George Bernard Shaw's, "Arms and the Man." We performed at different locales Thursday through Sunday for four consecutive weeks. Another production I was part of was "The Night of the Iguana" by Tennessee Williams. I was part of a gusto German family who wandered to the beach every act, singing German songs and otherwise being loud and obnoxious.

Being part of that German family was relief from the heavy dialogue of the rest of the play. But before the play, I had to put Coppertone sunless tanning lotion over all of my body. When I got home, I soaked in the bathtub to get the Coppertone off. However, one night after the performance, I was too tired to take a bath and just went to bed. I awakened in the morning to find my sheets covered with Coppertone. The Coppertone wouldn't wash out of the sheets even with hot soapy water and bleach. I learned my lesson never to do that again!

When I wasn't busy acting, I took piano lessons. Piano lessons were at seven o'clock on Monday nights at Miss Norma B. Taylor's home in Davenport, Iowa. Miss Taylor had suffered a severe case of polio in her earlier years. She walked with leg braces on both legs and had a slight limp as one foot was more difficult to move than the other. She earned a respectable living by giving piano lessons in her parents' home. She was an excellent piano teacher and I respected her tenacity very, very much.

Mom drove both my sister and me to Miss Taylor's house for our weekly sessions. Madeleine's piano lesson was first and mine was second. Sometimes, we also practiced duets.

Miss Taylor knew when we had not practiced enough. She was subtle in saying a particular piece needed lots more work. At the annual spring recital, Madeleine and I each performed a solo number without sheet music. Near the end of the recital, we played our duet. I think Dad was proud of us. He had wanted to take piano lessons in Germany, but for whatever reason he never did. Consequently, he insisted that his daughters take piano lessons.

When I was around sixteen years old, my parents informed me of some family history. My father's sister, who lived in Germany, was the only family member with blond hair and blue eyes, like mine. She and my father's brother both had manic depression, or bipolar disorder. They had severe episodes in their thirties and forties. As soon as I heard this, I decided to do my traveling while I was still young. In retrospect, that was a good decision.

Around the same time, I passed my Iowa driver's license test. My parents had been my driving teachers. Our mailbox was less than one-half mile away from the farmhouse. Sometimes, when Dad or Mom picked my sister and me up from school, we'd stop to pick up the mail at the end of the long driveway. Whomever was driving would switch places with me once we got to the mailbox; i.e., I would then take over the driver's seat and drive the rest of the way home. I was only ten years old, and Mom was teaching me how to drive her 1930 Model A Ford—stick shift and all! She was a very good teacher. She taught me how to release the clutch, how to shift without jerking, the importance of keeping both hands on the steering wheel, and how to make the turn into the lane by the farmhouse.

Shortly thereafter, Dad decided it was time to switch places in the car with Madeleine so that she could drive to the farmhouse from the mailbox, too. This was the first time she ever drove a car. I held my breath from the backseat. Unfortunately for Madeleine (and the car), she promptly drove the vehicle straight toward a shallow ditch. Dad had to think quickly. He immediately turned the steering wheel so that we were back on the road again. Needless to say, he took over from there.

Once I got my driver's license, I was able to start staying after school for my favorite clubs. One was called Tri-Y; it was affiliated with the YWCA. The other club was a bowling group. It was affiliated with the girls' recreation association. I also used the family car to take my sister and Alice Maxwell's daughter, Maggie, to monthly 4-H Club meetings in another 4-H Club member's home, as well as to 4-H softball practices and games.

The 4-H symbol stands for Head, Heart, Health, and Hands. From the age of ten until eighteen, I was a member of the Hickory Grove Blue Belles 4-H Club. Meetings were held once a month. The members of the 4-H Club gave talks and presentations with the assistance of two 4-H Club leaders. During my years in 4-H, I was elected as photographer, secretary, treasurer, and president. Being president gave me power and authority. Giving talks and presentations, as well as being president, taught me never to be afraid of talking in front of a group again.

Our 4-H Club often had its own exhibit at the Mississippi Valley Fair. These exhibits were on a rotational basis and included sewing and clothing, foods and nutrition, and upholstering and refinishing furniture. For example, all talks and presentations were on foods and nutrition if that was our 4-H exhibit for the year. My mother was proficient in all of these activities. She was a very good teacher.

Alice Maxwell, Mom's niece, sent her two daughters, Maggie and Maria, to my mother to learn how to sew. In learning to sew at different times in our lives, Maggie, Maria, and I didn't always sew our seams straight. When we messed up, we had to carefully pick the seams open—which wasn't a lot of fun—before pressing the fabric and sewing the seams again.

I remember when my Hickory Grove Blue Belles girls' 4-H softball team once won the county championship. I played second base, and Uncle Clarence Paustian was the coach. When I was at bat, I hit the ball toward the lower centerfield—high enough for the opposing second baseman and centerfielder not to catch it. My big hit allowed two runs to come in, and it also resulted in our championship win. I was ecstatic at my hit into centerfield.

When I was thirteen or fourteen, a twin-engine airplane crashed near our house on Uncle Clarence's land. I could see nothing but fire-red out either window. It had been a rainy, hot, and humid summer night. Dad quickly got dressed and moved his tractor and combine to the corner of the oats field. The heat from the fiery crash had scorched the paint on the combine. That evening, Scott County Sheriff Walt Beuse asked to use our telephone. He walked across the house toward the telephone, not even so much as removing his boots. Needless to say, Mom wasn't too happy cleaning up his muddy mess. The next day, citizens wandered over to the wreckage where body parts were still all over the place. It was a horrible sight that I will never forget.

When I was eighteen and my sister was sixteen, I noticed how much my sister was beginning to boss my mother around at one of my mother's parties. I detested my mother being treated this way, and I didn't like my sister becoming so bossy all of a sudden. It got to be too much for me, and I didn't want to cause a scene by yelling at my sister, so I went upstairs to cool down. Shortly thereafter, Alice Maxwell came upstairs to see how I was doing. I think she could tell I was upset.

"Joann, it's all right when you're alone with your mother, isn't it?" she asked me quietly.

"Yes," I replied. Alice nodded and went back downstairs.

I thought about the situation as I sat there by myself. My parents were the only people who could have broken Madeleine of her bossiness. I was disappointed that they didn't take the initiative to confront Madeleine's inappropriate behavior. I felt helpless because I knew I couldn't change my sister. Whatever the outcome, I had to live with it—whether I liked it or not. I wondered if my sister was lashing out because my parents expected her to do as well in school as I had. I felt very sorry for Madeleine because my parents placed that pressure on her, which she didn't deserve. I noticed resentment from my sister. A dear cousin said that my sister began to compete with the entire world.

I remember a time when we were in high school, and my sister came into my bedroom for clothes to borrow for the next day. However, I was never allowed to go into her bedroom. I was also forbidden to wear any of her clothes. Sometimes, I felt that because I did so well in school, I was therefore emotionally independent. But that was not the case. My sister once hit me on the head with a full-fledged hammer when I was five and she was three. Naturally, she was reprimanded for that. However, I doubt my parents were aware of the extent of the sibling rivalry between us. Whenever I asked Madeleine about her hostility toward our relationship, she always brushed off the topic, saying we could discuss it some other day. That was always her answer whenever I brought it up. To this day, no discussion has transpired. There can be no resolution without communication.

Looking back, I think my whole family could've benefited from better communication in general. Another memory I have is that we all would take turns showering in the basement at the farmhouse. After I took my shower and got dressed into clean clothes, I went upstairs to the kitchen where everyone else was. My father was sitting at the table in the kitchen. As soon as he saw me, he gestured with his hands to suppress my bosom. He did this many times. I didn't ask him why he motioned at me this way for fear of questioning his authority. Strangely, my father never did this to my sister. *What is he trying to tell me?* I wondered. *Does he wish I had been born a son instead?* Well, nevertheless, my bosom was much larger than my sister's—and I was okay with that. Some years later, during an appointment with my psychiatrist, Dr. Sidecar, I brought up the awkward incidents. "Joann," he stated emphatically. "You are your father's daughter and not his castrated son."

I spent ninth grade at J.B. Young Junior High School in Davenport. On a Monday night in March, I attended a roller skating party. It was fun at first, but then I suddenly became very ill. I headed to the restroom and began vomiting profusely. I reported to school like normal on Tuesday and Wednesday. The sickness came back, however, and I stayed home from school on Thursday and Friday. On Saturday, I was still not feeling my best. The next day, I felt like I couldn't leave my bed except to use the bathroom. Early Sunday evening, my mother decided it was time to call our family doctor. The family doctor came to our farmhouse to check on me. That's when I was told that I needed to be taken to Mercy Hospital immediately.

The doctors performed an emergency appendectomy around midnight. I was in the hospital for a week, and then I had to rest at home for a week. During this time, a classmate brought my schoolbooks home for me. I was able to finish my algebra assignments while I healed from the surgery. The algebra assignments were on addition, subtraction, multiplication, and division of algebraic fractions. When I returned to school, I simply submitted all of my algebra assignments to the teacher so that I wouldn't be so far behind the other students.

Throughout the day, my teacher taught five algebra classes. With friends in every one of the five classes, I found out that she had praised me in all five of her classes while I was on leave. Her compliment made me feel great because everyone knew this particular teacher was not quick to praise anyone. Later, my algebra teacher made sure I was signed up for geometry. This newfound confidence, thanks to my teacher, helped me realize that I could succeed in mathematics, and that no one was going to stop me. I even tutored Madeleine in geometry until she fully understood it. In later years, I was able to meet up with my wonderful algebra teacher and thank her for what she had done for me in high school.

Because of my appendectomy in the ninth grade, I was forbidden to drive a tractor in the field on the farm. Instead, my sister inherited the job of helping my father with fieldwork in the springtime. My job was usually mowing the grass in the yard around the house, in the barnyard, and in the orchard. I also trimmed bushes, cleaned windows, and did whatever else my parents assigned me to do. But even when I had done a good job mowing the grass, my mother would mow part of the grass again. This did not please me because I knew I had done a good job of mowing the grass . . . the first time.

After my sister graduated from the University of Iowa with several years of teaching experience, my father said to me, "Madeleine had a better college education than you. She is also a better teacher than you." Furthermore, he told me that I was abnormal. I said nothing back to him. I knew it wasn't true, but the fact that I had to listen to him degrade me was mind-boggling. However, what Dad said only strengthened my resolve. With time, I would show him what I was made of and what I could accomplish.

When my relatives or acquaintances sold me short, I just listened and thought to myself, *I'll show you what I'm made of!* I felt this way many times, and I think that kept me from letting my bipolar disorder get the best of me. I also found strength in tutoring others. I was really good at it. And later when I returned to high school and college reunions, I was slightly overwhelmed by the number of students I had tutored in mathematics. That was a good thing, indeed!

I started feeling very emotional during my junior and senior years of high school. In fact, I often cried myself to sleep at night. I don't know why I'd start crying. *Am I unhappy?* I wondered. *Am I suffering from the lack of attention my father paid to me?* I couldn't quite pinpoint the exact reason for these overwhelming emotions. I tried to shrug it off and concentrate on my studies.

My American history teacher at Davenport High School was Mr. Boyd Collins, a very interesting and unique teacher. He was well ahead of his time. His vocabulary was so extensive that I didn't know the meaning of most of the words he used. So, I spelled them phonetically, and looked at the spelling and meaning of the word from a collegiate dictionary at home. Expanding my vocabulary was fun. Mr. Collins's classroom style was quite different, too. Students had to read from four or five different sources about an event in American history and then discuss the pros and cons of these sources in class. It was interesting to hear differing points of view from students before arriving to at least one point of consensus.

One day, we were discussing the Immigration Quota Act of 1920 when one student in class asked, "What good are immigrants, anyway?" This hit a raw nerve with me. Trembling and with a clear voice, I told the story of my father's life, from his serving in the German Army in World War I to building pontoons in Belgium and France at the end of World War I. Dad also made two journeys to the United States through Ellis Island, New York, in 1923 and 1930. After receiving his American citizenship, he would tell his daughters how life was better in America than Germany. Oranges could only be purchased in Germany at Christmastime. Cars were more prevalent in America than Germany. To the best of my knowledge, Dad voted in every election since obtaining his American citizenship. He coerced others to vote, too. He impressed his daughters about voting—a right he did not have in Germany. I told the class that perhaps a proud, grateful American was the example my father set.

The bell rang; class was over. As I left class, Mr. Collins, in a very fatherly gesture, placed his arm around my shoulder to let me know that I had done a good job speaking my mind. Subsequently, he found out where I lived and came to the farm to hunt pheasants. Of course, he always had a lengthy conversation with my father, who kept Mr. Collins abreast of where I was and what I was doing after I graduated. I'm sure I disappointed him by not majoring in American history in the end.

When I was around sixteen or seventeen years old, my head started playing games on me. One time, my head sloshed around like Jell-O. I had to lie down to alleviate the dizziness and pain. Another time, my head hurt all over—especially my temples. The only relief I could get was to place my head on a pillow in a dark room. It felt like a migraine, but worse. These incidents occurred frequently for a couple of years. But then they stopped entirely when I was twenty years old. Looking back, these incidents could have been related to my bipolar disorder. (Note that every description of how I felt when I had a bipolar episode is justified in the "Definitions and References" section at the end of this book.)

During one evening meal, Dad thought I wasn't eating enough. I know I didn't sass him, but I probably just gave

him a look out of the corner of my eye. I was attempting to lose thirty pounds before I went to college. I was still heavier than he was. My father suddenly hit me so hard that I could not rotate my neck at all. It took three chiropractic adjustments before I could move my neck properly again. He never apologized, and that lack of sympathy hurt even more than the physical pain he caused me. However, my mother did come to me to say he was sorry for what he had done. After that, I was sure my father was in a good mood before I talked to him. Even though sometimes he was harsher than he needed to be with me, I still knew that deep down, he truly did care about me.

The only other cruelty exhibited by my father was when the pigs escaped from the yard. Now, the pigs had just been weaned and my estimate was that each pig weighed around thirty pounds. When Dad caught the escaped pig, he turned the pig upside down and beat the back of its head against the ground until the pig's nostrils were flowing with blood. He then released the pig in the yard where it belonged. Such cruelty! It wasn't the pig's fault that it had escaped the yard.

It was not a forgone conclusion that I went to college. For two years, my parents argued most evenings while at the kitchen table about whether or not I could have the money to attend college. During my junior and senior years of high school, I really didn't know if I would be able to go. I remember my father once saying, "What do girls need to go to college for, anyway?" Nevertheless, my mother had the final say. She clenched her fist and slammed it on the table, saying, "Joann wants to go to college. The money is there, and now that's the end of it!" My mother ultimately paved the way for me to pursue a career, even with my bipolar disorder.

Chapter 3:

Cornell College

I knew that attending Cornell College in Mount Vernon, Iowa, would be the correct choice for me because I would have been "lost in the shuffle" at a larger university. When I was there, all professors at Cornell College had earned a PhD in their fields of study; there were no graduate assistants teaching classes in those days. Dr. Watson Davis earned his PhD in mathematics at the University of Chicago. He was such a fine person and a wonderful mathematics teacher. Dr. F. Alan DuVal earned his PhD in German at the University of Iowa; his doctoral dissertation was on the history of the Amana Colonies. Oftentimes on Saturdays, I spent part of the day over at the DuVals' classically beautiful home.

I performed some menial tasks at the DuVal residence, such as washing windows, but I spent most of my time there babysitting Anne, Dr. DuVal and his wife Louise's daughter. Anne loved to have her back rubbed before she went to sleep. Dr. and Mrs. DuVal were such fine, gentle, and outstanding people. I know that Dr. DuVal was slightly disappointed that I did not major in German. I had been his top German student during my freshman and sophomore years. Still, my mind was set on majoring in mathematics.

Only a small liberal arts college gives students a chance to really know some professors and their families. During my years at Cornell College, these types of relationships were as important to me as the academic work. Dr. Otis E. Young was a professor of education who gave some good advice to my class the last day we all met before graduation. "When you get in the teaching world," he said. "You'll think you have all the answers, but you won't."

My years at Cornell College went quickly. I felt like I was busy all the time. I maintained a three hundred-dollar academic scholarship every semester while I was there, and I also had a part-time job placing desserts on trays. During my sophomore year, I washed glasses with a brush-like device and also assumed one-half of a dormitory proctor job. During my junior year, I corrected freshmen students' mathematics homework papers. I also landed a full-time dormitory job. In my senior year, Mortar Board, an honorary academic society based on service, scholarship, and leadership to Cornell College, chose me to be a member. Parents were invited to the initiation ceremony without the designees knowing about it. What a surprise! Mom and Dad showed up for the ceremony and even brought me a present.

When I was twenty years old, my parents returned me to Cornell College after a long Christmas vacation. Dad seated Mom in the car and then came back to see me in my dormitory room. He knew I was troubled; I had become increasingly difficult for him to understand. He wasn't anticipating that I could have bipolar disorder like his brother and sister. "Whatever you do, Joann, never lose your faith in the Lord. You'll need it," He said quietly with a great deal of emotion in his voice and face. He impressed me immensely with his thoughtful words, and they have stayed in my mind ever since. In fact, whenever there have been rough spots or difficult times in my life, I have always come back to his words of advice.

I decided to enroll in an introductory art class during my freshman year of college. I earned an A, much to the chagrin of the art majors. I surprised myself in having talent in art. Like with mathematics, it was most gleeful and exciting to learn that I was talented at something else. But by the end of the second semester of my senior year, I was utterly exhausted. There were practice teaching opportunities that surrounded my college schedule. With practice teaching, I had to make up physics labs on my own on Saturdays. In addition, Cornell College paid me to teach a section of college algebra—my schedule permitting—because of the overflow in enrollment.

When I was twenty, I was involved in a crisis with my parents brought on by the construction of Interstate-80 through eastern Iowa. My parents' marriage crisis came with taking some land via eminent domain for Interstate-80. When my parents married, Dad took all of his life savings and applied it to the new farm homestead. Furthermore, he had farmed all the land since his marriage to my mother. Dad felt he couldn't fight the process of eminent domain because the one hundred-acre farm was all in my mother's name. Mom inherited eighty acres from her parents and bought twenty acres from a brother. In my mother's family, it was engrained into the children by their parents that if they inherited any land, they were to keep it in their own name.

One day, Mom came to me and asked me what to do. I flopped on the couch and groaned. She knew she had crossed the line with me, but I gave her an answer anyway. "Mom," I said, giving it to her straight. "Dad has stuck by you all these years; I expect you to do the same." As I mentioned earlier, whenever we went anywhere, my parents usually held hands. They had great affection for each other and were able to show that in front of their children. Even though I didn't say it to Mom, these thoughts were in my mind as I spoke to her.

The interstate highway system in Iowa was begun in Scott County in eastern Iowa. Once the route was established, every farmer along the route was paid $400 per acre. Those who lost the least amount of land were paid extra for crop damages, erecting a new fence along the interstate route, etc. What this amounted to was that farmers along the route did not obtain the same price per acre. That, in effect, put more squeeze on the farmers who lost more land. My parents held out for condemnation, as did five other farmers. The six farmers who held out for condemnation hired an attorney, but the attorney wasn't very good. An Iowa Highway Commission attorney escorted a group of six men to survey the six farms that held out for condemnation. Dad said one man spoke German. *Is this not a conflict of interest for the attorney to accompany the group of six men?* I wondered.

It was the summer of 1957 when I accompanied my parents to the petit jury room at the Scott County Courthouse in Davenport, Iowa. Dad brought along a notarized statement saying the one hundred-acre farm would sell for $80,000, according to the farm realtor, Gus Schneckloth. I was seated between my parents. When the attorney for the Iowa Highway Commission entered the room, I said, "If you take away fifty-seven acres from the one-hundred-acre farm, you take away 57 percent of its value." Dad handed him the notarized statement. There was neither comment nor rebuttal from the attorney. I then added, "If you take away more than half of a farmer's land, the farmer should be reinstated on a farm of equal value."

My father nodded at my words, and then spoke up in all sincerity. "And I work hard to send my daughter to college!" he said.

This was a very difficult time for my parents, and I did as much as I could to help. There was still neither comment nor rebuttal from the Iowa Highway Commission attorney. Our price was held the same in the condemnation process, but the other five farmers received less money. Some days later, a farm real estate salesman stopped at the farm and asked Dad where Alfred Thodt lived.

"What do you want to see Alfred Thodt for?" Dad asked cautiously.

"To sell a farm," the salesman replied. Dad said he would be interested in buying a farm.

The result was purchasing a 160-acre farm, including Duck Creek, in Blue Grass Township. There were twelve heirs to the 160-acre farm estate, so the price was down a bit because of the cash sale. My parents could make the cash payment. Clem Werner, my parents' attorney, told my father, "Max, you've got a damn good deal here."

The tenants on the 160-acre farm in Blue Grass Township have been with our family for a very long time. They keep abreast of current agricultural trends to increase productivity from the land. They have excellent soil conservation practices. They are fair, honest, and reliable people in their dealings. My parents and I are lucky to have them as tenants.

After the land was acquired for Interstate-80, one year was spent grading the roadway. The roadway was left idle the next year. The following year, the roadway was paved in concrete; a strong undercoating of gravel with meshed wire on the top was then added. In 1948, my father had won an Iowa Corn Growers Association award—with a yield of 148.16 bushels of corn per acre on a ten-acre tract of land—that earned him a $25 savings bond. That land is now under Interstate-80.

As the interstate highway system spread nationwide, there were many, many families affected by the routes the interstate took. My heart goes out to them. The process can only be described in two words: pure anguish.

Chapter 4:

Teaching at Burlington High School

Armed with a BA degree in mathematics from Cornell College, I found my first teaching job at Burlington High School in Burlington, Iowa. The first year there, I taught two classes of Algebra I and three classes of Algebra II. In my second year, I taught three classes of Honors Integrated Geometry and two classes of Algebra II. My Honors Integrated Geometry course encompassed both plane and solid geometry. Knowing that my students had talent, I made this the most difficult geometry class I had ever taught. Solid geometry proofs require three-dimensional perspective, and this is not easy to grasp.

Gary Thorpe was a polite, courteous student in my Honors Integrated Geometry class. After Gary graduated from Burlington High School, he went on to major in mathematics in college and later returned to teach mathematics at Burlington High School for his entire career. John Garden was another excellent student in my Honors Integrated Geometry class. I never had to correct his tests because he always received As on them. John was always very inquisitive. He wanted to know if I was going to teach high school mathematics for my entire career. I said that I wasn't sure. Then he wanted to know why I chose to teach mathematics. I told him the story of my ninth grade algebra teacher and the influence she had on me at J.B. Young Junior High School in Davenport, Iowa.

I made quite a few friends while teaching at Burlington High School. On one auspicious occasion, four teachers, including myself, and two spouses, gathered on a swampy island in the Mississippi River. We took a boat and brought along folding chairs and ice chests with refreshments that included beer and food. The island was owned by one of the teachers, Mrs. Dahl, and her husband, Hermann. The sole purpose of going to the island was to "christen" a newly built outhouse. When using the facility, we were lucky if no one else opened the door on us while we were doing our business. We told jokes, sang songs, and told stories amidst constant laughter. What a good time was had at that obscure location!

In 1961, my parents drove to Burlington to surprise me on my twenty-fourth birthday. Dad telephoned me in Burlington, disguising his voice. It took me a few minutes to realize who he was, but I finally figured out who was calling. We had a nice picnic in the middle of Crapo Park. Crapo Park is one of the most beautiful parks in Iowa. Trees are planted from many countries in the world, especially those native to the United States and the Orient. The trees are all identified with metal plates on the ground, along with the name of each country that is represented. The trees are planted in such a way that the hue of the leaves and bark always creates a picturesque setting in the park.

Mom was somewhat concerned that I was leaving Burlington to go teach overseas in Okinawa, Japan. Dad tried to calm her down. "Oh, she'll come home again. She just wants to see some of this world," he said reassuringly to her. My father understood the German wanderlust that had captivated me.

Most river cities in Iowa along the Mississippi River have some bluff territory. On one of these bluffs, Snake Alley was built with bricks and cobblestones. The hairpin turns are so sharp that it almost defies description. When it was time for my parents to head back home, I hugged them goodbye and got into my 1954 Ford four-door car. With the utmost of caution, I very slowly traversed Snake Alley, thinking about what was going to happen next in my life.

Leaving Burlington after two years to teach in Okinawa, I received the most interesting letter from the Burlington Superintendent of Schools. He said that I was most welcome to return to the Burlington Public Schools at any time that I desired. That meant a lot to me, especially as I was about to embark on a whole new journey.

Chapter 5:

Okinawa

In the summer of 1961, when I was still a student at Cornell College, I heard about teaching overseas with the United States Department of Defense Dependents' Schools. In order to qualify for this, among other things, one had to have at least two years of teaching experience in the continental United States. I thought I might try it out. I had hopes to visit my father's relatives in Germany, especially my Aunt Ria. My Aunt Ria was the only sibling of my father who had blond hair and blue eyes such as myself. My father frequently mentioned the similarities between she and I. As fate would have it, she passed away before I could get to Germany.

The process of qualifying for the overseas teaching assignment included an interview held in Cedar Falls, Iowa. I brought with me many government papers that I was asked to complete before the interview. When asked for a preference of country, I said Germany. However, I was later informed that my locations would be Okinawa or Kindley Air Force Base in Bermuda. I chose Okinawa because I didn't want to teach in a junior high school in Bermuda. Furthermore, Okinawa gave me greater travel opportunities. Later, it was brought to my attention that the Kindley Air Force Base assignment in Bermuda was the most difficult overseas teaching assignment to obtain.

The same summer that I heard about the overseas opportunity, I took a short course in computer programming and a longer course in probability and statistics at Case Western Reserve University in Cleveland, Ohio, under the auspices of the National Science Foundation. I thought the classes would help me prepare for the trip to Okinawa.

Then came the news that I was going to teach five geometry classes in Okinawa at Kubasaki American High School, which was near the Naha Air Force Base. The chalkboards there were not useful at all; they were green painted slate boards. They were impossible to erase between classes. Instead, I came to school early to get all the geometric proofs on the board for each day's assignments.

There were five converted army barracks that composed Kubasaki American High School and Junior High School. There was a six-foot floor fan in each classroom to circulate the heat and humidity. There was no air-conditioning! Female teachers were allowed to wear canvas shoes with no hosiery. When in the classroom, it was nearly impossible for me to speak above the jets taking off on the nearby runway of Naha Air Force Base. There was quite a lineup of school buses that brought students to Kubasaki Senior and Junior High Schools. The busses transported students basically from Kadena Air Force along the way to Naha Air Force Base. The speed limit was thirty miles per hour on Okinawa because of the slow-moving horse-drawn vehicles and because children had no playgrounds—except for the streets.

What do Okinawans do for fun? Well, I got to experience what it's like to witness a habu-mongoose fight. Who ultimately wins? Okinawans place a habu—a poisonous snake—and a mongoose in a rectangular wire cage. Spectators pay a nominal fee to the Okinawan. The mongoose is so quick that it is able to sever the fangs of the habu before the habu can strike.

Another interesting sight I came across while in Okinawa was Suicide Cliff. It was neat in structure because it was a combination of coral reef and volcanic residue. It was at Suicide Cliff that the Japanese generals took their lives at the end of World War II. The Itoman rope was gargantuan, and the Itoman tug-of-war was even more interesting to witness. I also got to explore sugarcane fields in the southern part of Okinawa. I saw the burned-off sugarcane being brought in to the factory. I also watched it get processed to a brown state, or raw sugar. After it was processed, it was then sent to a refinery in Japan.

One day, I was walking downtown in the city of Naha when I came across a Communist rally in the street. I was jeered at, and I got out of there as fast as I could. Several teachers and I then decided to drive up to Nago, on the northern part of the island of Okinawa. We rented bicycles, toured the countryside, and saw Okinawan women tending the terraced rice paddies. Pineapple was also grown there. Several teachers dined at Harborview Open Mess in Naha and played slot machines there.

I was introduced to a woman named Michiko. Michiko was a dressmaker who made clothes for several teachers. On one occasion, I went to her to have clothes fitted. While I waited outside Michiko's small house, I noticed an Okinawan boy bouncing a volleyball in the street; he had no other place to play. When the other teachers and I left Michiko's home, I looked back and noticed the Okinawan boy was still playing. I wondered how many boards high I was and how much further he had to grow to be as tall as I was.

Okinawans tended to stare at me wherever I went because I am five feet ten inches tall and full-bodied. The Okinawans are shorter than the Japanese and have coarser hair than them, too. Since my hair was blond, the Okinawans kept looking at my head because I was different. They had not seen blond hair before, and my hair was extra blond from the intense heat of the sun. I let the Okinawans touch my hair whenever someone asked; they were very gracious when they touched my hair.

During my vacation time on Okinawa, several of the teachers and I traveled to the Philippines, Kuala Lumpur, Thailand, Taiwan, Hong Kong, and Japan, and Singapore. Singapore has such tall, straight palm trees. While in Singapore, Mary Ann, a junior high mathematics teacher who lived in the room next to mine, and I dined at a British restaurant. Two United States military men joined us at the table some time later. The conversation was interesting and polite, and I enjoyed the dancing. At the stroke of midnight, "God Save the Queen" by the Sex Pistols was played. The men picked up the tab at the end of the night, and Mary Ann and I were on our way.

"Jeepnies"—brightly decorated World War II jeeps—were in abundance as taxis. Mary Ann and I hailed one to go back to the hotel. The market square, which was filled with concession stands during the day, was totally vacant at that hour. Mary Ann decided to hop out of the jeepney to walk to the hotel. The jeepney driver, who wore a full turban and had a full black beard, pulled over to let her out. I hesitated to get out of the vehicle, but when the driver's beady eyes started to look at me, I jumped out, too. I didn't want to be carried off to Tippecanoe. We quickly paid the jeepney driver and walked the rest of the way to the hotel. When we arrived, the hotel attendant was sleeping on a cot in the lobby. He woke up and offered to take us up to our floor in a rope-pulled lift. We declined, saying we'd take the stairs instead. As we started to climb the stairs, however, the hotel attendant started chasing us! We ran for our lives, got in our hotel room on the third floor, locked it, and pushed as much furniture as we could against the locked door.

Other adventures while overseas included visiting the palace of the Sultan of Kuala Lumpur. Bangkok was interesting, too. The other teachers and I saw lots of Buddhists in their bright orange attire. On one day, several of us rented a small Mercedes van to travel north of Bangkok. There was only one road north of Bangkok, and rice paddies were on both sides of the road. We saw water buffaloes that were being tended to by their masters—young boys who often slept on the buffaloes' backs. Ultimately, we wanted to see the temple ruins in the provincial capital of Ayudhya in Siam. Tourist travel was closed in Cambodia; we could not see the temple ruins at Angkor Wat.

What I saw of Saigon was very brief because the other teachers and I were kept in a single terminal. I could see armed United States soldiers standing by helicopters on both sides of the new runway. Taiwan's Sun Moon Lake had a most unusual, extraordinary setting and color tone; it was a volcanic lake. Hong Kong had its outstanding restaurants and unique fashion. While crossing the Inland Sea from Kyushu Island to Honshu Island in Japan was vigorous, the other activities we did were great. We saw the Osaka Castle, the Imperial Palace of Kyoto, and the cities of Yokohama and Tokyo. Sadly, the Japanese did not open their palaces and shrines for tourists to see within.

My time on Okinawa was going great. However, there was a brief scare when Typhoon Tilda came at us—hard. Rain pelted the island and torrential winds clocked at 120 miles per hour came from two directions. The eye of the typhoon passed over us in approximately one-and-a-half hours, but then we still had to endure another ten or twelve hours of the typhoon and its aftermath.

During the storm, one inebriated United States Marine came over for a tray of ice cubes. The forty-man bachelors' office quarters (BOQ) in which the teachers lived were only one story high. The BOQ was like a small hotel: long and narrow with four floors and a corridor running down the middle of each floor. Every occupant was an employee of the United States government. For each occupant there were two rooms, a living room-sitting room combination, and a bedroom. And, of course, there was a shower and restroom facilities. The walls of the BOQ were made of cement blocks that were reinforced with interior steel beam supports. That didn't mean anything for Typhoon Tilda! The wind of the typhoon picked up a large rock and smashed it through a BOQ window. It didn't matter that the windows were steel framed with half-inch thick glass.

A bedroom was at each corner of the BOQ. There were two showers, a kitchen, and a living room with bamboo furniture in the middle of each one. But, most importantly, there was a laundry room with a washer and dryer and two large tubs with a washboard where our Okinawan maids washed and ironed our clothes in addition to keeping the BOQ tidy. I was the designated devil's food cake baker; I always used a Duncan Hines cake mix. The Duncan Hines cake mixes arrived in Okinawa fresh, but all of the other cake mixes arrived stale.

The local high school gymnasium was used as a large parking garage, so to speak, so that vehicles could be protected from the typhoon. Yet, during the calm and still after the eye of the typhoon passed, I could see vehicles battered around that had not made it to a garage. It was impossible to keep the rain outside the BOQ. We stuffed blankets in every nook and cranny where the water kept seeping in. Still, when the typhoon was over, the BOQ floor was completely flooded.

After the typhoon, when school was finally in session again, students needed to bring their own drinking water to their classes. I remember one student bringing his drinking water in a Jim Beam bottle. It was definitely an odd sight, but I didn't say anything. The students had already gone through enough.

One of my classes was Honors Geometry. The students in this class surprised me on my birthday with a birthday party, complete with cake, ice cream, and soda for everyone. The supervising principal told two of my teaching friends that she had finally found someone who could teach geometry! Before I left Okinawa, this supervising principal gave me her mother-of-pearl Tori Gate pin, which resembled the Greek letter, "pi." *Sayonara, Okinawa!* I thought. It was nice to feel so welcomed and appreciated.

The journey to Okinawa was definitely noteworthy. My footlockers were deposited at the Rock Island Arsenal and shipped to Okinawa in the Ryukyu Islands. I traveled by train from Davenport, Iowa, to California. My sleeper car was one car ahead of the caboose. As we whipped through the mountains, so did I in my sleeper. From California, we flew by Military Air Transport Service plane (MATS) to Anchorage, Alaska, for refueling. Such beautiful snow covered the mountains in Alaska. Our journey continued through the night on our way to Kadena Air Force Base in Okinawa. I sat near one of the turbo prop engines on the MATS. Suddenly, I saw redness that looked like fire coming from the engine. This brought me ten sheets to the wind!

Upon arrival, my principal met me and transported me to my living quarters. All the while, I was supposed to choose a maid. I was beginning to think I was going berserk, but then I remembered that I had had not slept since I left Davenport! As I napped for I don't even know how long, several teachers looked in on me to see if I was still alive.

The return journey to the continental United States was just as memorable. We flew by MATS again from Kadena Air Force Base to Tachikawa Air Force Base in Japan. What a rough landing! We were on the ground for four-and-a-half hours because an engine had been feathered; it had to be replaced. Then the journey continued to Wake Island for another refueling. From the air, Wake Island looked like a horseshoe, with one-half of it being runway space. Albatrosses were in abundance on Wake Island, building their nests at the end of the runways and simulating planes in flight. On one occasion, right before my eyes, an albatross that apparently had such poor depth vision landed in a shallow pond of water and came to a screeching halt. It was Woody Woodpecker all over again. No wonder Americans call them "gooney birds."

After one-and-a-half hours on the ground for refueling, we were finally airborne again. But not for long! Someone noticed the right wing was completely covered with fuel. This time, I was completely green in the gills. *Is my life ending now?* I wondered, trying not to lose it. The pilot immediately turned around and landed at Wake Island again. This time, the aircraft was refueled and the cap was properly placed on the fuel tank. Today, whenever I'm about to takeoff in an airplane, I lean back in my seat, close my eyes, and recite the Bible passage, "Nevertheless, not my will, but thine, be done."

We continued our journey to the Hickam Air Force Base in Honolulu, Hawaii. I disembarked there to take in the festivities of King Kamehameha Day, the Polynesian Cultural Center, shopping, walking, and just enjoying the climate. I left Oahu on a space available-basis in time to return to be there for my sister's wedding. Michiko had sewn my maid-of-honor dress in Okinawa.

Chapter 6:

My Sister's Wedding

Madeleine married Merle Sybil, whom she met while they were both students at the University of Iowa in Iowa City, Iowa. My sister majored in elementary education, and Merle majored in economics and business administration.

They were married in Holy Cross Lutheran Church in Davenport, Iowa, on June 23, 1967. However, their wedding did not proceed without a hitch. After the ceremony had begun, Otto entered the church with his ten-foot board that had lights on it to film the ceremony. No one hired Otto to come, but no one asked him to leave, either. With Otto's noisy contraption, I could barely hear my sister and her groom say their vows.

After the ceremony is over and the guests are all ushered out, it is customary for the bride and groom to leave to go to the reception in the backseat of a car; the best man drives and the maid-of-honor rides in the front seat. Instead, Merle drove the car with Madeleine in the front seat. Being the maid of honor, I sat in the backseat with the best man, waving to all the guests.

The reception was nice but it needed a band for dancing; it needed to be livened up, somehow. I noticed that neither my parents nor Madeleine and Merle for that matter were mingling with any of the guests. This was strange—at least for Dad—because when my parents usually went to a reception or a wedding anniversary, Mom would stay near wherever she was first seated but Dad, even with his thick German accent, circulated through the whole room and conversed with *everybody*. His social skills were awesome! So I decided to take it upon myself to mingle with the guests. Never did I have any problem talking to people and being cordial. Upon leaving, my beloved cousin, Margaret Kahl, told me she was so glad that I had visited with all the guests.

Madeleine taught in the upper elementary grades until her daughter, Marcy, was born. Once she had a baby, she was a stay-at-home mom. In fact, she didn't seek employment until after her son, Marlin, was in elementary school. Merle, on the other hand, worked in whatever capacities he was assigned at Collins Radio and Rockwell in Cedar Rapids, Iowa. He also decided to farm eighty acres of land with his other work assignment.

Marcy was designated a State of Iowa scholar when she graduated from Alburnett High School in Alburnett, Iowa. She majored in industrial engineering and graduated from Iowa State University in Ames, Iowa. A sorority sister of hers had me as a mathematics teacher at Bettendorf High School. This sorority sister reported that I talked about Marcy and Marlin as if they were my own children. Marcy likes to play softball.

Marlin majored in marketing and later graduated from Wartburg College in Waverly, Iowa. He likes to go hunting and fishing with his father. With a bow and arrow in hand, Marlin once killed a ten-point buck as a teenager. Marlin is a towering six feet four inches—or is it six feet five inches?—and enjoys playing a game of basketball.

Marcy and Marlin have always been polite, courteous, and thoughtful people. They are both productive, hard-working citizens. My sister and her husband are to be commended for producing such fine children.

Chapter 7:

My Niece's Wedding

My niece, Marcy, married Marcus Braun on June 29, 1996, at the chapel in Yosemite National Park in California. Marcus graduated from San Luis Obispo University, also in California, with a mechanical engineering degree. Yours truly was the pianist, playing Bach's "Ave Maria," the bridal chorus from "Lohengrin," and Mendelsohn's "Wedding March"—with no mistakes, I might add!

My sister proved to be quite a seamstress for her daughter's wedding. There were five bridesmaids in different parts of the country. Each bridesmaid sent Madeleine dimensions to work with. Madeleine, in turn, made inexpensive tea-length sample dresses for each bridesmaid and then sent them to the girls. The bridesmaids then tried on their gowns. They each pinned where their dresses were too large or indicated where they were too small. Once my sister received the altered samples, she was able to begin cutting into the lavender bridal fabric. In the end, the bridesmaid dresses all fit like a charm. After that, Madeleine began sewing dresses for other weddings, as well as elaborate draperies for homes.

My niece and Marcus are now the proud parents of two toddlers, a son named Joshie, and a daughter, Jessie. I remember that when Marcy was younger, she once asked her father if he thought she had enough patience to ever become a mother. Yes, she does.

Chapter 8:

Teaching Abroad

Before departing from McGuire Air Force Base for Europe, I spent several days in Washington, D.C. The Smithsonian Art Institute and the National Gallery of Arts were indeed impressive. After visiting the Lincoln Memorial and the Jefferson Memorial, and reading the inscriptions there, I realized that there was a lot of greatness in the United States. But my next teaching assignment was at Neu Ulm American Junior High School in Neu Ulm, Germany, and I was looking forward to what Germany had to offer, too.

The junior high school was held in converted German Army barracks, just bordering the United States Army pool area. So, again, there was much noise to contend with! In fact, I couldn't talk above the vehicles at the United States Army Third Infantry Division. Most of the children had a parent who was a non-commissioned officer. My first year's teaching experience there included two sections of seventh grade math, two sections of eighth grade math, one section of ninth grade algebra, and two sections of girls' physical education. Teaching girls' physical education proved to be quite an experience. I did the exercises and calisthenics with the students, but I was not prepared for the seventh grade girls taking showers in the presence of each other. As I recall, all of them were late to their next classes.

On the other hand, seventh grade boys are something else. Some of the students I taught didn't know whether to think of themselves as mice or men. There is such variety in junior high students. They can be organized or not, considerate or not, polite or not, punctual in their assignments or not, airheads or not, attentive or not, etc. Since I had never taught in a junior high school before, I can honestly say that it takes a special personality to be a junior high teacher. My hat goes off to all junior high school teachers out there!

After my first year of teaching junior high school students, I wrote a letter to the superintendent of the Southern Area Command, asking to be relieved of my girls' physical education teaching assignment. I was qualified for the position simply because I was female. In my second year at Neu Ulm American Junior High School, I taught two sections of English, two sections of seventh grade math, two sections of seventh grade literature, and one section of ninth grade algebra. Wouldn't you know it? I wasn't even certified to teach seventh grade English, seventh grade literature, or girls' physical education. How these schools meet North Central Association accreditation, I'll never know. Teachers' meetings in Munich tended to be gripe sessions. Teachers often (loudly) wondered why they were assigned to teach certain subjects when they were certified in completely non-related subjects.

Shortly after I sent the letter to the superintendent, I was asked to report to a doctor at Augsburg Air Force Base after school on Mondays. I don't know who recommended that I report there. The doctor and I discussed a variety of things, but to this day, I'm still not sure what the actual purpose of these brief meetings was. However, on the sixth visit, the doctor asked me if I could ever love a man. Completely confused, I replied, "Why, of course!" After that, the doctor told me that I didn't have to come and see him anymore. In retrospect, I wonder if these meetings were because of the letter I wrote to the superintendent saying that I was qualified by sex only to teach girls' physical education.

The opportunity for travel in Europe was tremendous. Two Okinawa schoolteachers—Mary Ann, who taught in Orleans, France, in 1962 and 1963, and Clarise, who taught in Aschaffenburg, Germany, in the same years—joined me in Munich for the Oktoberfest parade. The Oktoberfest parade filled the spirit of the occasion. Bleachers were set up along the parade route to accommodate the large crowd, but fees were charged for anyone who wanted to sit in a bleacher seat. The mayor of Munich participated in the parade; he was in a horse-drawn open black carriage laden with lots and lots of yellow roses.

There were lots of beer wagons carrying many barrels of beer in the parade, each from a different brewery. The wagons were pulled by horses that were adorned with shiny brass plates of armor. Performers representing each province of Germany were clothed in native dress and either performed a little dance, skit, or some kind of special routine. I stepped back when I saw a clown, but he saw me step back, and presented me with a coal smudge on my nose. All the Germans around me laughed. There were also three imposters who pretended to make ammunition but they never did. Their routine was similar to something the Three Stooges would've done.

After the parade, the teachers and I headed to the huge beer tents that were set up in a large park. In the center of one of the beer tents was a stage where the Oompah Band played. Surrounding the stage were rows and rows of tables for people to sit at after they ordered beer. Only liters of beer were served. The waitresses impressed me. Some of them carried three liters of beer in each hand to their customers! Bratwurst and Brötchen were the best tasting foods to counteract the beer. How many liters of beer did I have that day? How should I remember that? My friends and I just wandered from tent to tent to see if the spirit was the same at each one. The Germans sang with such gusto! Yes, they *definitely* enjoy their beer.

During Thanksgiving vacation, I took the train to visit my German relatives in the towns of Laboe and Neu Heikendorf in the northernmost province in Germany of Schleswig-Holstein. My relatives welcomed me warmly. However, I wasn't quite sure how my head would react to a whole day of speaking German. My brain often hurt after a full day of speaking the language. But in the morning after a good night's sleep, my brain was usually free of pain. The Sunday after Thanksgiving was Totensontag, or Memorial Day, in Germany. We paid our respects at the cemetery for Aunt Ria. My German relatives knew that my parents and I would be visiting during my summer vacation.

Eating food, German-style, requires the fork to remain in the left hand rather than switching it to the right hand as in America. When meat is cut with a knife, the knife is used to anchor the meat on the fork before it is consumed. The whole meal is consumed in this way. The evening meal, or Abendbrot, was done in the same manner. A slice of bread was placed on a plate, or Abendbrotbrett (evening bread board), and margarine would be applied. Then the bread would be topped with cheese, sausage, or smoked fish. The same fork and knife routine followed. Germans never eat sandwiches with their hands.

The week before Thanksgiving on a Friday, New Ulm teachers Marge and Zoe and I ate dinner at a Weinerwald, a chicken rotisserie restaurant. We returned to our rooms at about eight o'clock at night. When I was in my room, I generally had the Armed Forces Network radio station on. That evening, I heard that President John F. Kennedy had been assassinated. All residents of the forty-man BOQ where I lived in Neu Ulm stayed up all night at the shock and utter disbelief of the assassination.

There was no school in Neu Ulm on the Monday of President Kennedy's funeral. We had satellite coverage for part of the proceedings. Our satellite coverage ended when Jackie Kennedy walked between Robert F. Kennedy and Teddy Kennedy. On the United States Army Base in Neu Ulm, there was a fifty-gun salute at five o'clock in the evening. One of my German cousins had taped President Kennedy's "Ich bin ein Berliner" speech, which transpired in Berlin. As I visited with my German relatives and read the newspapers, I came to realize the high regard in which President Kennedy was held.

On the Thanksgiving weekend that followed the assassination, several of the Neu Ulm teachers began their journey on the Orient-Express in Ulm, Germany. We arrived by train in

Budapest, Hungary. Lots of construction was taking place, and there were many female construction workers around.

We were invited to a Hungarian elementary school. In every classroom, there was a bulletin board with a picture of Jack Ruby killing Lee Harvey Oswald posted on it. No translator was there for the Americans and Hungarians. The Hungarian teachers spoke to their students. I felt so squeamish and humiliated at the way the Americans were being treated.

As we approached the Hungarian passenger rail car, we noticed the railroad car was filled with other passengers. The Hungarian officials had to remove those passengers from the railroad passenger car. As the passengers left, they jeered at us and made faces at us. European passenger cars have an aisle down one side and compartments seating eight on the other side of the aisle. Three people decided to stay on in my compartment.

A Hungarian gentleman in his early to mid-twenties sat diagonally across from me near the middle of the compartment. He was making his first trip outside Hungary to visit a relative in Vienna, Austria. There were five Americans in the compartment, but everyone spoke German. At first, the conversation was very casual. Whenever we traveled behind the so-called Iron Curtain, we brought American cigarettes, Hershey's chocolates, and copies of *TIME* magazine with us. This young man looked around all the time as if he feared that someone was spying on him. Gradually, he loosened up, however, and even took a Hershey's chocolate.

The conversation continued. I finally found the nerve to ask the young man a question. "Sind die ungarische Leute mit ihrer Regierung zufrieden?" I asked, offering him an American cigarette. ("Are the Hungarian people satisfied with their government?")

He accepted the cigarette. Just then, the train pulled into the Vienna station. The young man helped me with my coat. As we stood next to each other, he replied, "Es ist nicht zu sagen dass es anders sein konnte, aber wir konnen nicht wählen." ("It is not to say that it couldn't be different, but we cannot vote.") As I thought about it later, I came to the conclusion that one day the Berlin Wall would fall—and in 1989 it did!

During the first weekend in May, I went to Holland with my Neu Ulm teacher friends, Zoe and Gladys, to see the tulips in bloom. However, yours truly was the driver, and we got involved in a five-car pile-up on the autobahn near Stuttgart. The fourth car in front of me literally stopped dead in its tracks. My car was eventually taken to a body shop in Stuttgart, and the three of us then journeyed to Neu Ulm by train. The following weekend, the three of us journeyed successfully to Holland in a different vehicle.

There were fields upon fields of bright red tulips in bloom in the Netherlands for as far as the eye could see. What an awesome sight it was! We passed homes with their spring finery on display. It was almost like there was a parade float bedecked with flowers in front of each home, similar to floats that would be at the Rose Parade. We also toured Kuekenhof Gardens and stopped at the Ryksmuseum in Amsterdam.

During my second year at Neu Ulm American Junior High School, I noticed that my seventh grade math class was not at the typical seventh grade math level. There were so many new students that year that had come from the southern United States. Using math educational materials from the teachers at Neu Ulm American Elementary School, I was able to obtain my students' proper placement. There was a small group at a seventh grade math level, a much larger group at a fifth grade math level, and one student at a third grade math level. The student who was at a third grade math level should have been in special education classrooms to help him with his learning needs; however, this was not an available option. I did the best I could in accommodating all groups. It took a lot of planning and organization on my part! I insisted that all groups work quietly. Activities were planned for all groups each school day. When one group would be quizzing or testing, I would be teaching another group a new topic and helping them with their homework. It worked extremely well because they were cooperative and willing to learn once they were in the right math groups.

During spring vacation, four tour buses transported American schoolteachers from Nuremburg, Germany, to Moscow, Russia. Some American schoolteachers flew to Moscow first and then returned to Germany by bus. An Intourist guide accompanied us everywhere during the trip. The Mercedes Benz tour buses were very modernistic; i.e., the tops of the buses were encased in glass. Many native citizens stopped to study the tour buses. Our first overnight stop was in Prague, Czechoslovakia. As we continued our journey to Warsaw, Poland, the next day, a large rock from an approaching military truck smashed the windshield on the driver's side of our tour bus. Our tour bus driver replaced the windshield with a Plexiglass one, and we were on our way again. We traveled on two-lane concrete roadways that sometimes became gravel for a stretch. The only other vehicles we saw belonged to the military. Passenger car traffic was more or less confined to the cities.

The next day was Easter Sunday, and we were free to plan our days as we wanted. A couple of teachers and I decided to go to the church where Cardinal Wyzinski was preaching. It was a cold and rainy day; parishioners wore their woolen coats that were dusted with rain. The smell of humanity permeated the air. There was not enough seating for the parishioners, so many of them stood in the aisles and at the back of the church. When mass concluded, it looked like just as many parishioners had arrived for the next mass. It was heartwarming to see the Polish people in such great attendance.

Later that day, our bus approached the Polish border with the Soviet Union. I didn't realize how thorough the security check would be! We disembarked from the bus, and our luggage was placed on a table. We all had to stand before the table while the border guards inspected our luggage. We also had to exchange our dollars for rubles while we were at the border; currency couldn't be exchanged elsewhere. We then traveled to Minsk, the capital of Byleorussia—or Belarus. When our bus parked in front of the hotel we were going to stay at, it caused quite a bit of curiosity among the local citizens.

When I spoke German to one of the older gentlemen, the Intourist guide told me not to spoil their people. We all ate dinner and then relaxed for the rest of the evening. The next day, we would be journeying to Smolensk.

The trek in the Soviet Union to Smolensk felt like a paltry wintry one, even though it was early April. Mounds of snow could be seen everywhere. Even more surprising were the miles and miles of very high marsh grass. We must have been traveling through considerable marshlands. As we approached Smolensk, smoke stacks could be seen in the large industrial city. However, a beautiful Russian Orthodox Church dominated the skyline. As we disembarked by the hotel, four of us decided to go explore the church. We passed some factory workers, who were pedaling their sewing machines for every stitch. What a clatter those sewing machines made! We were warmly greeted as we approached the fence of the church courtyard.

The people at the beautiful church all spoke French, and we asked if we could be given a tour. I had never seen such gorgeous icons before! Several Russian families of church officials lived on the premises. After our tour was over, we bid a fond farewell. No other Russians greeted Americans as warmly as they did there. We ended up being late for our evening meal, but it was always the same: pommes frites, green peas, and always some form of steak.

We traveled to Moscow the next day, and we stayed at the Hotel Ukraine, a relatively new hotel made with green wood. The cracks in the flooring were very large, and carpet rugs covered some of these places. The plumbing in the bathroom in our room was truly a work of art. Three of the four walls in the bathroom were covered with tubes and pipes; it provided some comic relief. Rube Goldberg must have designed it!

In Moscow, we saw an evening performance of the Bolshoi Ballet. The following evening, we went to a show at the Moscow Circus. The audiences at these two events represented different segments of the population. While in Red Square, I passed by Vladimir Lenin's bier, making sure there were only Russians in front of me and behind me. It was interesting to observe them. We walked down a flight of stairs and entered. We then walked up a flight of stairs, passed the bier, and then walked down a flight of stairs before making an exit from Lenin's tomb. The Russians were so serious; it was as if they were in a communion line in an American church. Men removed their hats and placed them over their hearts as they passed by the body of Lenin.

From Lenin's tomb, I journeyed into GUM, the state department store. It was a very ornate building with some interesting things on display. One could buy a bar of soap made with lye. Women's underwear was about fifty years behind the times; lingerie was not yet a part of their vocabulary. St. Bartholomew's Church in Red Square gave no one access because all entrances and exits were boarded up. We were promised a visit to a Russian school, but the authorities we had spoken with rescinded on the deal.

We saw long lines of people standing with empty jars in their hands. They were waiting to have them filled with sauerkraut by ungloved hands (under the most unsanitary of conditions). As many times as I rode the elevators in the Hotel Ukraine, I often wondered what countries were represented where we were staying. Any place else but Moscow, people would have been at each other's throat, wouldn't they? One parting thought on Moscow: The grandeur of the subways was palatial.

We flew from Moscow to St. Petersburg aboard an Aeroflot plane, whose cabin door was not quite closed. Personnel were standing nearby so the cabin door wouldn't fall out. Upon arrival in St. Petersburg, we visited the Hermitage Museum, a complete museum in every sense of the word: art history, musical history, history of the literature greats, and the complete governmental history of Russia and the Soviet Union. A replica of St. Peter's Basilica stood in St. Petersburg for the sole purpose of ridiculing all religions on the face of the earth. The Roman Catholic Church was pictured with a cardinal, a bishop, and a monsignor in their elaborate robes and implying the clergy lived upon their parishioners. Cars driven in St. Petersburg reminded me of a 1954 Ford four-door sedan. I passed a church with wood stored in it. An eighty-year-old woman (in my estimation), dressed entirely in black, walked over and touched the trickling water to cross herself and pray. What a poignant end to our journey.

From St. Petersburg, we flew to Prague next. We then had a bus tour of Prague and later continued journeying to Nuremburg. Over President's Day, Marge and I took a train to Zermatt to see the Matterhorn. The train was a different one; it made so many stops! I called it the "milk train." Unfortunately, the cloud cover over the Matterhorn never diminished the whole weekend. C'est la vie.

During the first Christmas vacation in Germany, I decided to take a trip to the Holy Land with the Geisler Travel Service. Twenty-three teachers were on this trip. We flew by Yugoslavian Airways to Athens, Greece, where we had half a day to explore and gaze at the majesty of the hill where the Acropolis and the Parthenon stood. The other half-day was spent in Turkey. There, we got to see the Blue Mosque in Istanbul, with its circular ring of bulbs emanating from the center of the ceiling until about ten feet from the floor.

The next day, we journeyed to Cairo, Egypt, to a large museum that contained mummies and other Egyptian artifacts. We shopped for the rest of the afternoon. Many young children rode sidesaddle on camels or on their fathers' shoulders. So many of these young children only had one eye. *What disease causes the loss of one eye?* I wondered. We wandered to the slum areas of Cairo. They were not a pretty sight. In fact, they were the worst slums I had ever seen. Litter was everywhere. A lot of the shacks were made of flimsy tin. Meanwhile, poor children played everywhere.

The following day, we took a camel ride in front of the Great Sphinx and the pyramids, including the Great Pyramid at Giza. I had never rode atop a camel before; I didn't even know how to mount it! First, I took a photograph of the camel that I was supposed to ride. Its head was adorned with brightly colored decorations that were absolutely stunning. However, while I got close enough to the camel's head, I had to be careful not to get spat on! When the camel was lying down, with its legs tucked underneath its body, I awkwardly mounted the saddle on its back. Then I clung to the saddle for dear life. When the camel slowly rose to its front feet first, I really had to hang on tight so that I wouldn't fall off. Then the hind legs came up, making me more or less parallel with the ground. The ride was not smooth, but jerky. The most important picture to take is of the camel owner atop his camel. When I was comfortable in my saddle, I asked the camel owner to take a picture of me and the camel I was on. I handed the man my camera with the same settings I had been using to snap other photographs. The picture with the camel driver had come out excellent; the picture of me on the camel was very faint in color. Go figure.

That evening, a few of the teachers and I were invited to a tent party in the Sahara Desert at the invitation of four Danish pilots and their stewardesses. No stewardesses came, but there were some Egyptian men present. They were all smoking a water pipe. The teachers and I stuck together and left after a short period of time. We were tired. The previous night, we had been invited to an Egyptian nightclub with lots of belly dancing. Performances were very interesting, to say the least. What is it about Arab men that they can't keep their hands off blond-haired, blue-eyed women?

Next, we visited the cities of Luxor, Karnak, and Thebes, all located on the Nile River. Luxor is the city of the living with its palatial estates and hotels. Karnak is the city of worship, with its many ornate columns and Egyptian hieroglyphics. Thebes is the city of the dead. While there, we walked down to King Tut's tomb. King Tut's tomb was filled with intricacies of detail everywhere. The motif was all in black and gold. *Magnificent!* I thought as I quietly took in all the wonder around me.

Cedars of Lebanon trees were abundant. The city of Beirut was not yet under siege, as it would be in years to come. Along a street in Damascus, Syria, a horse was carrying a huge basket of live crabs for sale. They didn't look a bit appetizing! We stayed in the Jordanian half of Jerusalem. Toward dusk, we journeyed over the hills of Judea to Bethlehem where we saw the place where Jesus was born. While there, I also attended a German Lutheran church service on Christmas Eve. Later, we journeyed back to our hotel in Jerusalem.

Our next stop was in Nicosia, Cyprus, to visit a neutral country before going to Israel. We landed in Tel Aviv, saw Jaffa, went to the port city of Haifa, and ended our day at the Dead Sea. An Israeli tour guide accompanied us on our long bus ride to all of the different locations. He talked practically all the time about the merits of Israel. The casual observer could notice standards of agriculture far and above any of the Arab countries. The closer we got to Tel Aviv, the more tired we became of the Israeli tour guide. To shake things up a bit, the twenty-three of us suddenly began singing, "God Bless America." We sang in sincere, genuine, and harmonious voices, and the tour guide *finally* quieted down. I think he was flabbergasted by the whole situation. What a memorable moment to end the trip! The next day, we had to fly back to Frankfurt, Germany.

What were my final thoughts on the Holy Land? The tourist guides in each country were not enthusiastic about their jobs. It was as if they had repeated everything they did and said one too many times; they had seen too many tourists already. I left the Holy Land with the distinct impression that the only thing holy was the sacred ground on which historic events had occurred.

One spring vacation, my Neu Ulm teacher friend, Gladys, and I decided to travel to Yugoslavia. We took my car and drove to a point in Austria where we could park the car and then board a train. The train took us through the mountains to a place in northern Italy. Then we continued our journey by going to the Adriatic Sea. We took a boat and headed off to Dubrovnik, a quaint village on a mountaintop in Yugoslavia. The boat captain tried to have both of us pay twice for the boat ride, but he did not succeed.

Dubrovnik was an artist's colony with a venue of shops. We went on a bus tour of the beautiful city. At one stop, a van of gypsies drove by us, hooting and hollering. We took many walks while we explored Dubrovnik. The scent of fresh spring flowers was overwhelming, but in a good way. Finally, we took the train back to Rijeka to find my car where we had parked it. Luckily, there was no apparent vandalism to it.

Several weeks before my parents came to Germany for seven weeks, my teacher friends from my Okinawa days, Clarice and Mary Ann, met up with me in Paris, France. We viewed Paris from the top of the Eiffel Tower, had a boat excursion on the River Seine, saw the Left Bank, and marveled at the Arch de Triumph, its many feeder streets, traffic congestion, and lack of accidents. Walking down the Champs-Elysees, we encountered a man who was sweeping the street with a long-handled, slanted broom. While we were also in Paris, we had to indulge in strawberries and cream—and we paid for it later, too! Our days were jam-packed. We visited the Louvre Museum, making sure we saw the *Mona Lisa* painting and *Venus de Milo* statue, among other famous pieces of art. We also went to numerous patisseries and marveled at the colored chalk artistry on the concrete surrounding Sacre Coeur Cathedral in the Montmartre District.

The next stop was Orleans where Mary Ann had taught at Orleans American High School. Statues depicting Joan of Arc mounted on a horse were visible everywhere. The largest of these statues had a special nickname given by the Americans: "Joanie on the Pony." Nearby, there was another large sculpture that was nicknamed "Dottie on the Potty." Apparently, soldiers dubbed the statue that funny name in 1962.

Next, we traveled to Bordeaux and thought it would be fun to stay at a campground. I slept on the ground in a sleeping bag. There was only one little problem: I was longer than the sleeping bag! I ended up resting my chin on my forearm; that was my makeshift pillow. In the morning, I discovered that some insect had bitten me on the lip, leaving a weird-looking red bump.

After our brief camping excursion in Bordeaux, we journeyed to Madrid. The Imperial Palace was impressive. We enjoyed a little shopping during the day. At night, we dined at a restaurant called Botin's. Botin's house special was "roast suckling pig." It was actually a superb meal!

Toledo was next on our agenda. Very interesting! El Greco, a famous painter, sculptor, and architect of the Spanish Renaissance, did his masterful work in Toledo. After we had gotten our fill of Toledo, we headed off toward Barcelona. We noticed so many buses, vans, and other vehicles that were filled with men going in the same direction as us. Later, we learned that there was a big soccer match in Barcelona that day. Needless to say, there was not a room available at any inn we stopped at. We stayed near one hotel so that we could use the restroom facilities whenever we needed to. Otherwise, we spent the afternoon shopping and taking in the sights.

Soon enough, it was time to keep going. Clarice drove in the rain for two hours. When it was my turn to drive, I had no idea what I was in for. It was nighttime. I crossed the Pyrenees through Andorra. The so-called road was extremely narrow with long planks that were anchored by the mountains. It was not a smooth ride, and I had to keep my eyes focused to cross at the middle of the planks. I drove only ten or fifteen miles per hour, too afraid to go off a cliff—especially with my driving history. I was glad that Clarice and Mary Ann were fast asleep in the backseat of the Volkswagen Beetle. It took me approximately three-and-a-half hours to cross the mountain. Finally, I reached the Spanish-French border, which just so happened to be closed to vehicular traffic.

Mary Ann continued to sleep in the car for a few hours. Clarice and I awkwardly got dressed for the next day before climbing into our sleeping bags and falling asleep, too. The night patrolman was looking for Mary Ann. She, of course, was still sleeping in the car. When the Spanish workers reported to work in France early in the morning, all fingers pointed at the three of us. I had worn a muumuu on top of my regular clothes in my sleeping bag. When I crawled out of my sleeping bag, everyone was staring at me in my disheveled glory. Carefully, I removed my muumuu, only to reveal a new set of clothes underneath! I think some of the men were quite disappointed. I tried not to laugh at their expressions. Well, that was the end of our crazy little journey together. I needed a shower, my clothes needed to be washed, and I needed to prepare myself for my parents' arrival.

I excitedly met my parents at the Frankfurt International Airport. After our hellos and hugs, we headed to the northern most province in Germany, Schleswig-Holstein. We had family members who lived in Neu Heikendorf, and another set of family members lived in Laboe. Of my father's five siblings, two had joined him in America; two lived in Germany; and his older brother, Peter, was killed in World War I. My father and his sister Maria, or Ria for short, were born less than a year apart from each other. In fact, they were in the same grade in school. Aunt Ria passed away slightly more than a year before my parents got there. Her husband, Uncle Hermann Rühr, was still alive. Hermann and Ria had two sons. Max, was almost ten years older than me, and Klaus, who was about three years older than me. Max married a woman named Ruth Kankowski, and they had three children: Silke, Jens, and Sabine. My father's oldest sister was Emilia, but everyone affectionately referred to her as Emmy. She married the widower, Heinz Artkämper, who had three children from his first marriage. Heinz and Emmy had a son, Peter, who was born in the same year I was. Peter was a special cousin of mine, like a long-lost brother.

My parents and I stayed in Aunt Emmy's apartment. It was Dad's duty to go to the bakery every morning to buy Brötchen (fresh hard rolls) and Semmeln (fresh lightly sugared rolls). One would never know when he would return; he always seemed to find several people to engage in conversation with. Whenever he would return, we would all have our continental breakfast—rolls, margarine, jam, and coffee—and then get ready to start the day.

Every day brought a new journey. First, we visited the cemeteries in Laboe and Neu Heikendorf. A florist's shop was conveniently located by one of the cemetery entrances so that fresh flowers could be purchased and placed around gravesites. Germans decorate their cemetery plots much like flower gardens, complete with very low shrubbery. Some folks get creative with rocks. I once saw some cemetery plots in Neu Ulm that were artistic works of stone with just a few flowers here and there.

On another adventure, we decided to stroll in the sand at one of the German beaches. Later, we sat and relaxed in a strandkorb, or a beach basket. Strandkorbs are unique to that part of Germany on the Baltic Sea. It seats two and can be rotated for as little or as much sun as the occupants want. The cover provides an excellent windbreak. Once we were ready to go again, we took off to go visit das Ehrenmal (the Memorial) in Laboe.

Inside das Ehrenmal, we learned all about the history of the German Navy in both World War I and World War II. We also saw a giant U-boat—a German World War II submarine—in front of das Ehrenmal that was anchored in the sand. A little while later, We took an elevator ride to the top of das Ehrenmal. The view from the top was breathtaking! We got to see a panoramic view of the region known as Probstei. In early June, the fields of Probstei are in bright yellow bloom. Dad said rapps seed were planted, which then grew into plants that produced these bright yellow blooms. When harvested by combine, tiny black seeds were produced. Storks followed the threshing combines to eat the tiny seeds before going back to their nests at the top of cross-sectional brick chimneys. Dad said the rappes seed was used for margarine, or it may be linseed oil. I don't know which.

After two weeks in northern Germany, my parents and I headed to other parts of Europe. Near Kassel, we had to stop at an American gas station to get some fuel for my car. Meanwhile, Dad wandered off toward the snack bar. He returned with a strawberry milkshake and a cheeseburger. I chuckled to myself. He didn't realize how much of an American he had become!

Our next excursion was between Bingen and Koblenz, the picturesque gorge on the Rhein River. We couldn't have asked for more wonderful weather. Then we went to my quarters in Neu Ulm to wash our clothes. The washing machine was located in the basement, and later I would bring the clean clothing to the fourth floor to dry. Unfortunately, there was no dryer in the basement.

After our clothes had been washed, my mother was standing on a four-footed stool to hang clothes on the curtain rod when she suddenly lost her balance and broke her left wrist. It was too late in the day to go to the emergency room so my mother iced her wrist and took it easy for the rest of the night. We really wanted to watch the Ulmer Boat Parade; however, and found spots on the banks of the Danube River to take it in, resplendent in its multi-colored pageantry. The Danube is neither that wide nor that deep in Ulm. But, what a spectacular boat parade it was with gigantic water sprays and colors everywhere!

The next morning, Mom's wrist was really hurting. We brought her to the emergency room where we found out it was definitely broken. With Mom's wrist in a brace, we then decided to go visit the three castles of "mad" King Ludwig: Neuschwanstein, Herrenchiemsee, and Linderhof. Neuschwanstein is most often photographed from the air because it is perched so high in the Bavarian Alps. I call it the fairytale castle because of its view from the ground. Herrenchiemsee is on an island in Lake Chiemsee, the largest lake in Germany. The castle has a hall of mirrors like in the Versailles Palace. Violin concerts by candlelight were given on Saturday evenings, weather permitting. Linderhof was the most exquisite of the three castles. There was water rushing down the Italian steps, so named because of an Italian replica. A flower-filled French courtyard at the Linderhof was also created as a replica of a courtyard in France. There was even a peacock throne on the premises. According to history, King Ludwig dined alone with food brought up from a clap door in the basement of that castle.

On a nice summer's day, my parents and I journeyed through Austria and came upon a massive mountain. It was none other than Die Zugspitze, just from the Austrian side. An immense meadow sprawled out before the mountain. The entire sight took our breath away. We continued our trek through part of Austria and Vaduz, Liechtenstein. Die Zugspitze is the highest mountain in the Bavarian Alps. Then we went on to Garmisch-Partenkirchen in Germany with all of the quaint murals on its buildings.

Mom, Dad, and I took an underground salt mine tour in Garmisch-Partenkirchen. I had never gone on a salt mine tour before. In the winter, when I was in Garmisch-Partenkirchen, my surroundings were majestic. The roofs on the buildings had to be extremely strong to support all the snow! Overall, Mom liked Switzerland the best. We first went to Bregenz, Switzerland, where musical chimes and music boxes were made. Then we drove the Klausen Pass, where there was open grazing for cows, goats, and sheep. Each cow had a cowbell around its neck. The animals were tame; Dad stood right next to them, and they were never frightened.

We headed back to Neu Ulm to wash our clothes before going back to Northern Germany for two more weeks. Whether separated by the Atlantic Ocean or not, family is family. I felt so at home when I was with my German relatives. We talked all the time. Topics of conversation included politics, global issues, and economics, to name a few subjects. However, Hollywood movie stars are not the same as

German movie stars, so we didn't talk about that. My German relatives' humor and speech was similar to how my mother's family in Iowa was. Aunt Emmy always talked of courage when she spoke about the two World Wars.

During World War II, Germany got its food supply from the Sudetenland. When the war was over, food was difficult to come by. Aunt Emmy talked about cooking cow beets in so many different ways just for a meal. My parents sent many food packages, containing powdered milk, packaged puddings, Hershey's chocolates, sugar, and most importantly, roast beef canned in gravy. Dad and Mom canned the roast beef in gravy all by themselves.

It seemed like we took some kind of road trip in the area each day. With two cars, the Stuhr and Rühr families went to Denmark and southern Sweden. Uncle Hermann loved the Danish rolls just as much as we did. In Denmark, there were heavy burlap sacks containing barley. At the end of the day, the burlap sacks were left in the field. My cousin, Peter, exclaimed, "This could never happen in Germany because the Germans would steal the sacks of barley!"

We climbed the circular staircase in a small castle near Malmo, Sweden. On the return trip to Germany, Americans could bring as much Danish butter back with them as they wanted to, but the Germans were limited. They didn't check my car with United States plates, but they checked the car at the Danish-German border with German plates. Again, in awe, Peter said, "They believe the Americans, but not the Germans." Even though time passed so quickly, the memories that were created are still so vividly great.

On the way to the Frankfurt International Airport for my parents' return to Iowa, our car got a flat tire on the autobahn. Time was short, and a German man was so kind to stop and help us so that we could be on our way again. Mom later wrote me a postcard saying that she and Dad would remember these days for the rest of their lives.

I returned to Neu Ulm just in time for the beginning of school there. The second year, I taught seventh grade

English, seventh grade literature only two days a week, one section of ninth grade algebra, and two sections of seventh grade math. I grouped the students to what grade level they were at, and the process was as successful as it had been the previous year.

One Wednesday after school, Beth and I drove in Beth's Kharmann Ghia to the Canadian Air Force Base PX in Baden Baden, Germany. Camera equipment, sewing machines, and typewriters were much cheaper there than at the American stores. I bought Zeiss Ikon camera equipment and a Singer sewing machine. I don't recall exactly what Beth bought, but she purchased some camera equipment, for sure.

On our way back to Neu Ulm, I was driving Beth's Kharmann Ghia and suddenly got lost on the detours surrounding the Stuttgart Hauptbahnhof railway station. The railway station was one-way only and one block long. Several streets ran into the street in front of the railway station. Of course, I went the wrong way in front of the railway station. A policeman in his car saw me do this, even though there were no other cars to be seen anywhere. The policeman pulled us over and spoke to me in German. I answered in English in such a way that if the policeman actually understood English, he would not have been able to understand me. This went on for some time until the policeman finally shrugged his shoulders, went to his car, and left. Beth and I left, too. We drove in silence for a few minutes. After several blocks, however, we stopped and howled with laughter. In no way was I going to take the rap on this infraction!

Chapter 9:

Graduate School

Traveling abroad had been an amazing experience, but it was soon time for me to attend graduate school. I shipped all of my possessions back to the United States in two crates. The larger one would be stored in my parents' attic, and the smaller one would be sent to the Sage Graduate Center at Cornell University in Ithaca, New York. I also had to ship my car from Bremenhaven, Germany, to Newark, New Jersey. Naturally, with my luck, I picked up my car to find dents in all four fenders.

I had received a National Science Foundation academic-year scholarship to study mathematics. I took regular mathematics course offerings at Cornell, no diluted courses whatsoever. Some students from the eastern states were irritated when I did better than they did on exams—and we took a lot of exams.

Cornell University was very well staffed. There were enough graduate assistants to correct a weekly homework set for each course. I never worked so hard in my life, but it was good for me. I took a very different kind of abstract algebra course from a professor who was also writing a book on the subject. It was very interesting and a good course. I also took a calculus course from a matrix algebra perspective. I had never taken a class like it before, and I was thrilled when I scored 100 percent on the final exam.

School days were always pleasant. Whether at the Fairview Number Three one-room country schoolhouse, J. B. Young Junior High School, Davenport High School, Cornell College, or Cornell University, I performed very well. Every school day was a positive experience. As time progressed, my self-esteem, my self-confidence, and my self-worth soared.

Besides, I felt like I had to show the world what made me tick.

While at Cornell University, I made friends with a few fellow graduate students. One student there, Margaret, once told me that I needed mental health treatment. I said nothing in response; instead, I just silently absorbed her words. However, another student, Patricia, invited me to her home in the Bronx over Thanksgiving. It was a really nice gesture.

On the Wednesday before Thanksgiving, Patricia and I both had exams to take, but Patricia's exams were scheduled earlier in the day than mine. I gave her my extra set of car keys so she could bring her luggage to my car in the student parking lot while she waited for me. When I finally got to the parking lot with my own luggage, the car was all loaded and ready to go. But that's when I noticed that Patricia had placed my car keys on the air vent. I should have grabbed the keys as soon as I saw them, but I didn't. As we journeyed along, the car keys slipped into the air vent from the heater, never to be seen again.

The journey from Ithaca to New York City passes over the Catskill Mountains. Driving my Volkswagen Beetle with a stick shift, I often had to shift from fourth gear to third gear whenever I was going up a hill. One time, when I was going up a hill and shifting from fourth gear to third gear, the knob on the stick shift fell off. On top of that, it began to rain as we approached the Palisades State Parkway in New Jersey. My windshield wipers didn't work, either. We stopped at a service station, but the workers there didn't know how to repair the wipers. When I got back into the car, I grabbed my long-handled squeegee. Patricia made a face like she had no idea what I was about to do.

As we crossed the double-decker George Washington Bridge toward the Bronx, I stuck my hand out the window and awkwardly used the squeegee to clean the windshield so that I could see my way across the bridge. When we finally got to Patricia's home, we both breathed a collective sigh of relief. That evening, I checked my headlights; they didn't work, either! Patricia and I decided to go to the city and see a play performed in German at the Lincoln Center. We figured it would be a better idea to take the New York City Transit System instead of my crippled Volkswagen Beetle. The play featured Ernst Deutsch, Germany's leading actor. As I sat in the Lincoln Center, I noticed the resemblance of the walls to what I had seen in the Vienna State Opera House.

On Thanksgiving morning, Patricia and I eagerly went to see Macy's Thanksgiving Parade. No television coverage can do justice to the parade compared to seeing it firsthand from the sidewalk. The giant floats were like large skyscrapers. Indeed, it was all a majestic sight to behold. After the parade, we spent time with Patricia's family and helped wherever we could to get the turkey and all its trimmings prepared. Thanksgiving dinner was later in the afternoon, and it was splendid and bountiful, to say the least. I experienced such fine hospitality while at Patricia's home. When we could no longer put food into our mouths, we drove back to Cornell University.

In 1965, it was not that easy to get a teaching job, even after receiving a master of arts in teaching degree from Cornell University. My job hunt was pretty much confined to upstate New York. I accepted a job at Mohawk Valley Community College in Utica; it was going to be a difficult year. The college had initiated a new Liberal Arts Math course, but no one had actually set it up yet. Liberal Arts Math students contained those who had one year of algebra and one year of geometry, two years of algebra and one year of geometry, two years of algebra, or one year of geometry and one year of trigonometry. With such a broad spectrum of student backgrounds, how could one set up a course, let alone be successful at it?

I began with matrices with regards to addition, subtraction, and multiplication. Complaints kept coming in from the confused students, even though they all had had this in a different form in one year of algebra. I also dealt with dice and simple probability. However, it was a no-win situation. The students in my Probability and Statistics were supportive of my teaching, as well as the Secretarial Science students who were in their second year of algebra, but everyone else remained frustrated.

It was four o'clock in the afternoon before the day I was supposed to give my Liberal Arts Math exam. I stayed at school to compose and type it. Around midnight, when it was completed, I went outside to my car. It was plowed under, even though I had a sticker on my windshield that requested for it *not* to be plowed in. It's nothing for it to snow twenty inches in one fell swoop in Utica. Whenever that happens, a lot of drivers tie red handkerchiefs to the antennas of their vehicles so that other cars can see them. I finally got my car free, went home to get some sleep, and then returned to school by seven o'clock the next morning with a pile of exam printouts in my hands, all ready for distribution.

My decision not to return to Mohawk Valley Community College the following year was precipitated by neither a salary increase nor the impossibility of making Liberal Arts Math a viable course for college credit. That summer, I attended a National Science Foundation Institute for twenty-one teachers of calculus at the University of Georgia in Athens, Georgia. Fortunately, we had an air-conditioned building where we could meet for classes, as well as study in the evening. I found this training very beneficial, especially in later years when I taught calculus again.

I sent copies of my résumé to the community and regular colleges in the Pacific Northwest through the University of Washington. Soon, I had an interview in the fenced backyard of a University of Idaho math professor's home in Moscow, Idaho. Two huge boxers roamed freely during the interview. My mind was spinning as the professor went over the terms. I was to receive less money than in Utica to teach three classes of calculus and work on my doctorate. *Is this even a good deal?* I wondered. Furthermore, he didn't discuss the most important issue with me: There was to be an increase of six hundred students at the school. At the same time, there were no plans to create new dormitories, and student apartments were already at a premium price. *I'd be crazy to accept this offer,* I thought as I got back into my car that afternoon. Ultimately, I declined the job offer at the University of Idaho.

After reprioritizing my life, I decided to leave Moscow and head toward Lewiston, Idaho, on a Saturday. The morning when I decided to take off was sunny and bright. The wheat fields in the Rocky Mountain Plateau country had just been harvested; I felt good. My new car—only ten days old—was packed to the hilt. I drove along the road for a little while, taking in the sights and sounds.

Suddenly, out of the tall grass in a ditch, jumped a mature female mule deer. She tried to jump over my car, but she didn't make it. Instead, her front hooves came through the windshield, directly in front of the steering wheel! The force of the impact threw her off my car, and her rear quarters then caved in my right door—glass and all. I managed to keep my car under control by steering it onto the shoulder of the road. I could see that the back of the mule deer was broken. For the longest time, I spit glass from my mouth. Even though my sunglasses protected my eyes from the shattered glass, I could feel pieces of glass everywhere.

The couple in the car behind me was most helpful. They immediately pulled over after they saw what happened. The man removed all of the loose glass that he could, which included the front windshield and the glass in the right front door. The closest Volkswagen body shop was located in Lewiston. The couple told me that they would follow me to Lewiston to make sure I got there safely. Little did I know that I would be driving fifteen miles down the infamous Lewiston Hill—totally hairpin turns! I looked in the rearview mirror. I was definitely a sight to behold with my hair standing straight up from all the air space. One driver just about lost it when his vehicle met me as we both went around a bend. In fact, I'm pretty sure I frightened many people on the Lewiston Hill!

I found the body shop shortly before noon. The owner came out to my car before I even had a chance to turn the ignition off; clearly, he saw a woman in distress. I explained to him what had happened and then was graciously driven to a motel. The first thing I did when I opened the door to my room was take a shower to rinse all the glass shards off of me. Unfortunately, on top of the broken glass and body damage to my car, the mule deer had also defecated everywhere in all the commotion. I spent two weeks in Lewiston because the replacement windshield was backordered from Spokane, Washington. At least I was able to get weekly rates at the motel. I'd go to the body shop to get a status report every day while I was living in the little motel.

I did a little exploring while I waited for my car and found a YMCA in Lewiston that had a piano. I'd sometimes go there and play it to pass the time. I also had my sewing machine with me. The motel was air-conditioned and had a television, so that was nice. I later learned that Lewiston is on one side of the Snake River and Clarkston, Washington, is on the other side. This is the area where Evel Knievel made his famous jumps. The thought made me grin. After everything I had gone though, I kind of felt like Evel Knievel's long-lost relative.

It was storming a little bit when I left Lewiston for Vancouver, Washington, in my fixed car. In fact, the wind was blowing so hard that a random road sign suddenly flew in front of my vehicle. *You have to be kidding me!* I thought as my heart leaped out of my chest. Luckily, the sign missed me. I took a deep breath and tried to focus on the task at hand. I was headed to Clarice's parents' home where I would stay while I learned the ropes of my new career. I couldn't wait to try something other than teaching. I was ready for a challenge.

Chapter 10:

A New Career at Boeing

I had interviewed for a position as a scientific computer programmer at the Boeing Company in Seattle, Washington. Shortly after, I was offered the job. Being a scientific computer programmer was a brand new experience for me. This was in the days before there were computer science majors in college. To qualify for employment as a scientific computer programmer at Boeing, applicants had to meet the following criteria: a B in all college or university coursework and either a BA degree in mathematics or a BS degree in science. Those employed, including myself, were required to partake in an extensive course by Boeing to make sure our skills were comparable. Keep in mind that the deluge of computer science majors from colleges and universities came *after* 1966. Needless to say, my employment at Boeing was interesting. There was always so much more to learn!

I took computer-programming classes all day long during the first three weeks at my new job. The aerodynamicists, for whom I gave computer support, received uninstalled jet engine performance in the form of binary cards, or binary tape. The aerodynamicists then designed a nacelle, or configuration, around the uninstalled jet engine performance to produce the true performance of the jet engine. At one time, I had twenty-two different jet engine programs. The plot package was used to find climb, cruise, and takeoff graphs. Unfortunately, I'm not at liberty to say what else I did during my four years at Boeing; a lot of my work had to be kept confidential.

The big scare occurred after approximately two years of working at Boeing. I remember the day like it was yesterday. One Monday morning in 1968, when I was thirty-one years old, I reported for work as usual with the exception of not feeling very well. My head felt like slush, and it was difficult to focus on my work. I tried to concentrate but I wasn't myself; I found it difficult to keep on task with my head in so much pain. Tuesday presented the same picture with some added dizziness. When Wednesday came along, I didn't know what to do or where to go for help with my sudden depression. My head was in far greater pain than it had ever been in before.

My health deteriorated as the week progressed. I knew I wasn't very productive at work and was concerned about my job performance, which led me into an even deeper depression. This horrible feeling preyed on me in my weakened state. I knew I needed help. Not knowing what to do, I quietly laid down on a cot in the women's lounge to rest.

My next memory was waking up in a hospital. I had absolutely no recollection as to how I got there. Much to my amazement, I felt fine when I awoke in the strange hospital bed—but something was very wrong with me. What a scare! I was used to being so independent and in control. *What is going on with me?* I wondered. More importantly, would it happen again?

I had no idea how long I had been in the hospital. Doctors conducted a battery of tests, but it seemed like they couldn't come up with a proper diagnosis. *What will I do about work?* I wondered as the days went by. Luckily, Boeing allowed me to continue working on the condition that I find a psychiatrist. I chose to see Dr. Bauer.

Dr. Bauer put me on a medicine called Thorazine, which didn't make me feel any better. However, he was adamant about the drug. Quite frankly, I now know that Thorazine was the only drug psychiatrists had available back then. Dr. Bauer also told me that I was schizophrenic, but I didn't believe him. He wasn't convincing; I felt like he was just guessing what could be wrong with me. After two years with Dr. Bauer, I still didn't feel confident about his skills. I knew it was time to leave Seattle when he said I should ask my parents for money for his services.

I decided it was time to go back to teaching—what I knew best. I tried to find employment in the Seattle public school system but there were no vacancies. The Seattle area was full of people; jobs were scarce. Still, I didn't want to work as a computer programmer anymore. I resigned from my position and left the city. Interestingly, when Boeing hired me, the company had approximately one hundred thousand employees. When I left, there were only thirty thousand employees.

There were episodes before this one at Boeing. In 1967, an acquaintance of mine took me to the Seattle-Tacoma International Airport at Christmastime. I was on my way back to Iowa for the holidays. When I reached Iowa, my mother noticed that I was not quite acting like my usual self. I would talk a lot, and nothing made any sense. When I did this, I could never hear what I was saying. I also continuously paced the entire house, both upstairs and downstairs. I know now that these strange behaviors were attributes of my bipolar disorder.

Nervous, Mom called our family doctor, Dr. Schwarz, and asked him to come to the house as soon as possible. Dr. Schwarz drove to our home, took one look at me, and gave me injections in my arms. When that didn't help, Dad and my cousin, Leland, took me to the hospital. They had to place me in the middle of the front seat of the car so that I wouldn't try to jump out. I don't even know how long I had to be hospitalized. That night, my mother and father made a pact not to tell anybody about my health. My cousin didn't even tell his parents. He respectfully thought the issue was my parents to decide whether they shared the information or not.

Dad was adamant that we were going to keep my condition a secret. "We're not going to tell anybody about this!" he said. He wanted to free me of the stigma of bipolar disorder, which he knew so well from his own family. To this day, I've had more than one psychiatrist tell me of the importance of secrecy, with as few people as you can completely trust, in order to maintain some sort of a "normal" lifestyle.

Another time, I was hospitalized in One North at Mercy Hospital in Davenport, Iowa, at Christmastime again. Dr. Silos was my doctor this time. My parents, my sister, and Pastor Kitten came there to see me while I was hospitalized. My hospital stay was brief and without major treatment.

My life seemed somewhat normal for a little while, but then I suddenly began suffering from severe migraine headaches, which could only be relieved by lying on a soft pillow and having the shades drawn. Lying on a soft pillow could relieve sometimes-milder headaches on top of my head and in the temple area. Temple pain meant that I couldn't do anything but lie down until the pain subsided. Around the same time, I was told that I also had sleep disorder. Insomnia triggers bipolar disorder. I couldn't fall asleep because there were too many things crossing my mind. The frequencies of these conditions were becoming overwhelming. I decided it would be best to go back home to Iowa from Washington.

Even though I felt dizzy, I knew I had the strength to drive home if I took my time. My parents wanted me to call every evening to let them know where I was. They were worried about me; they knew I was not well. Deep down, my body was telling me the same thing. When I finally reached their house, I didn't care if I ever worked again.

I immediately took the initiative to call Dr. Erling at the Scott County Medical Society. I had been a former patient of his. I asked him for the name of the best psychiatrist in the Quad-City area, and he gave me the name of Dr. Sidecar. I immediately made an appointment with Dr. Sidecar, hoping that he would be able to help me. When I met Dr. Sidecar, he conducted a few tests, asked me a lot of questions, and decided that I was suffering from depression. Then he went to work, trying different medicines on me and studying their effects. After about nine months, I began to feel better. In fact, I even felt like trying to go back to work. My mother noticed that the medications were improving my well-being. She suggested that I take them for the rest of my life.

In retrospect, I consider the nine months I spent with my parents in Iowa a pivotal part of my life. Being around people who were supportive and working with Dr. Sidecar, who had genuine warmth and concern for my health, renewed my faith in myself. During those months, I did chores around the farm and even lost weight from being so active and trying to take better care of myself.

However, it was also around this time that my dad was placed into intensive care. He had been diagnosed with the beginning stages of colon cancer. Despite his own condition, he was glad to see me getting better. His demeanor had softened; he was not so critical of me anymore. In fact, I believe he felt badly that I had the same affliction that his sister and brother had. I knew it wasn't his fault. My parents were extremely supportive of my efforts to be well. They helped me rejuvenate my life.

Chapter 11:

Teaching at Bettendorf High School

After returning from Seattle in April 1970, I hadn't cared if I ever worked again, but that feeling didn't last long. Teaching seemed to be in my blood. Nine months later, I landed a job teaching mathematics at Bettendorf High School. I taught there for twenty-nine-and-a-half years. Luck was with me full-time!

During my tenure at Bettendorf High School, there was a long period of time when Dr. Sidecar only asked to see me once a year. None of my medications were changed. Dr. Sidecar always let me know when he wanted to see me. He also let me know when I needed to have a blood test so that he could test both my eskalith and creatinine levels. That was pretty much the way Dr. Sidecar operated—with one glaring exception.

I felt particularly edgy during one weekend. My speech just didn't sound right to me. I called Dr. Sidecar and left a message on his professional answering machine. My message must have sounded alarming to him because he appeared at my doorstep with medicine early Monday morning. He also instructed me to stay home from work for a few days. I faithfully stayed home from work and didn't drive my car for a full week. By the end of the week, my speech pattern was back to normal again.

I started teaching at Bettendorf High School in January 1971 to replace a teacher who moved from the Math Department to an administrative role. Monday, my first working day, turned out to be a snow day—no school. Since I still had so much difficulty sleeping, Dad took me to work the next day. He also picked me up when school was let out. When my father realized I had the same affliction as his sister and brother, he was much kinder to me than he had been in previous years. I now realize how much he cared, and it was a lot. I remember how happy Dad was when I told him that I got the teaching job.

For the last three weeks of the first semester and all of the second semester, I took over Dr. Leroy Moles' classes in beginning algebra, math analysis, and honors math analysis. Dr. Leroy Moles immediately became the assistant superintendent of schools of the Bettendorf Community School District. I was very fortunate to have the opportunity to get a job during the year; this was a nice bit of luck for me.

I always taught math analysis or pre-calculus, either regular or honors. Sometimes, I taught advanced algebra or geometry with the calculus and pre-calculus. Over time, I developed new units where the textbooks were weak. Advanced math, a semester of matrix algebra, and a semester of probability and statistics were replaced with an AP calculus course, following a statewide trend in Iowa.

The training I received was at the Institute for Teachers of Talented Students at Carleton College in Northfield, Minnesota. It consisted of four AP calculus summer workshops, and it was immensely helpful in developing my AP calculus curriculum. The workshops were on AP calculus AB, AP calculus BC, and two on graphing calculator usage in an AP calculus course. This began a long and continuing story of integrating technology into math instruction. Passing the AP calculus AB exam would earn a student one semester's college credit. Passing the AP calculus BC exam would earn a student two semester's college credit.

Both the AP calculus AB exam and the AP calculus BC exam now have calculator questions in them. Each of the four workshops was conducted in a similar format. In the mornings, the mathematics professor would give presentations and/or lectures. During the afternoons, we were assigned to work problems relative to each morning's presentation. At the end of each work session, we were given a homework assignment to do in the evening. On the last day of the workshop, we were asked to write a term paper that would be due at the end of the summer. The term paper had to use ideas of the workshop and correlate them as building blocks for the classroom. I can't imagine a teacher beginning to teach calculus without this beneficial training.

My mentor in advanced algebra at Bettendorf High School was Ken Horning. He was the truest friend I ever worked with in mathematics. He shared his expertise with those who asked him, as I did, and I became a much better teacher because of it. Ken was also a pleasant tease, sometimes writing my name as "Stewer" on memos. He had received his training under the late Henry Van Engen at the University of Northern Iowa in Cedar Falls, Iowa. Ken taught me how to write multiple-choice questions for exams by carefully choosing the wrong answers he thought students would make.

I often told Ken in later years that he earned some of my awards. Rudy Meier was a well-respected teacher who was instrumental in getting recognition or awards for me, too. There was a science teacher, Mr. Sandman, whose favorite pastime was giving both students and faculty members unique, clever nicknames. His nickname for me was "The Baroness von Stuhr." Sometimes, I heard my students say "Baroness" at the back of the room, but they'd never say it to my face. In return, some faculty members gave Mr. Sandman the nickname, "Donald Duck," because of his distinguished gait.

After my father died in 1975, I felt even more alone in the world. So when my cousin Peter Artkämper's widow, Annelisa, paid a visit to the United States, I was thrilled to have relatives see me at my home. Sadly, Peter and Annelisa were married less than a year when Peter passed away at the age of twenty-nine years. He had such pain in the abdomen that exploratory surgery was done, only to find an intestinal tract that looked fifty years old. But his heart did not survive the surgery. Earlier, when he was in the German Army, a separate surgery had showed part of his body was not beyond the fish gill stage. He was such a nice person and seemed like my long, lost brother.

When Annelisa came to Davenport, she stayed at the home of my Aunt Annie Stuhr Schuldt and her husband Henry, but she spent the weekends with me. Annelisa also visited my classes at Bettendorf High School. She'd stay entire days to watch my students learn. I recall her handwriting looked just like a typewriter font when she wrote comments about the students in my classes.

Annelisa was very interested in the culture of the United States. She really enjoyed observing my students and my teaching style. When she toured Bettendorf High School, she commented on how quickly I wrote on the chalkboard, like I was typing on a computer. She also commented on the good relationship I had with my students. I was thrilled to have her with me for her visit to the United States. While at my apartment, she once removed a slice of bread from a Wonder Bread package. "What is *this?*" she asked about the slice of bread. "It is so . . . gummy!" she continued. "The Germans are known for baking good breads of great variety with fiber."

On an autumn day, Annelisa, my mother, Aunt Annie, and I drove to Pikes Peak State Park in Iowa. Pikes Peak State Park is the highest elevation in Iowa, overlooking the Mississippi River. The purpose of the trip was to have a picnic in Pikes Peak State Park. As we journeyed along, we saw beautiful fall leaves everywhere. When we finally found a spot for our picnic, we sat down and began to spread everything out. However, it was so cold that we had to bundle up in all the clothes we had. That picnic ended up being the fastest one I had ever been a part of; we were chilled to the bone in a matter of minutes. Some picnic!

At Bettendorf High School, I was the one who was primarily responsible for curriculum development in the Math Department during the summer. One summer, two other advanced algebra teachers and I developed the curriculum for a new advanced algebra textbook. When I asked for their points-of-view, they agreed and supported mine. However, the other two advanced algebra teachers never once asked me for my support or opinion on what they had worked on. They only collaborated when I initiated, never the other way! I felt our working relationship would worsen if I pursued this one-sided situation. What causes a breech in a working relationship, anyway? Is it jealousy, arrogance, a feeling of superiority or something else? I wasn't quite sure.

The mathematics teachers at Bettendorf High School had meetings, as necessary. These meetings were referred to as "team meetings." None of them were more spirited than those regarding teaching assignments for the following school year. This was a situation where personalities came to the forefront. The stakes—the teaching assignments for the entire next year—were always high.

One of the algebra I teachers, Verla Funk, was a quiet woman of few words, but whenever she talked, everyone listened. Verla earned her master's degree from the University of Iowa, but she preferred to teach algebra I to freshmen and sophomores. "I don't consider myself any less of a teacher because of my choice," she once said. She also added, "Ken Horning and Joann Stuhr should be exempt from teaching general math courses because they have skills for upper level mathematics courses." Verla had a strong conviction about the best way to teach children. She was headstrong and always supported me. She was able to discern between being certified to teach a mathematics course and being qualified to teach a mathematics course. With her passing, being certified *and* being qualified lost some of its value.

You see, men mostly taught the upper level courses at Bettendorf High School when I first started working there. One teacher, Ronna, and I wanted to go to the Regional Conference of the Teachers of Mathematics in Omaha, Nebraska. However, our administrators preferred having a man drive the school station wagon. Ronna had just learned to drive a car and was terrified to drive across the Twin Bridges. The administrators let us go to Omaha in a school station wagon. I made sure I drove the whole way. Ronna and I talked during our drive. Suddenly, before my eyes I saw a sign that read: WELCOME TO MISSOURI. There was an Iowa map in the car. We had time, so we decided to take the back roads through Mt. Ayr and Red Oak on our way to Omaha.

There was one stretch of road that was three lanes wide; the middle lane was a passing lane. A semi-tractor trailer approached me in my lane, thinking he was in the passing lane. I immediately steered the school station wagon to the right-hand ditch because there was no other place to go. Ronna looked at me incredulously. "How did you know how to do that?" she asked. It took me several minutes to settle my nerves after that. When we finally arrived in Omaha, we found our hotel and parked the station wagon in the parking lot. After that little escapade on the three-lane road, we decided to walk wherever we could. We also decided to keep our little close encounter with a semi-tractor trailer a secret.

There was some envy by a few of the other teachers when I was moved to the upper-level classes. Men typically had held these classes before. As teachers of math retired or passed away, there was an influx of other kinds of math teachers. These teachers taught by memorization and did not attend mathematics-related conferences at the state, regional, or national levels to experience alternative methodologies of teaching. These teachers were not as prepared and did not attend summer mathematics training, either. Basically, they had no way of improving their knowledge of the subject. However, one exception was Ray Lort, who commuted by motorcycle to the University of Iowa to earn his master's degree in mathematics. Some teachers were a bit arrogant; they did not know or perhaps want to address the limitations of their mathematical skills. Others played politics with the principal for favorable course assignments.

What was my teaching style like? Well, I enjoyed teaching mathematics, and I enjoyed working with my students. I took the challenge of finding the motivation of each individual very seriously. From my own high school days, mathematics always gave me the greatest challenge, and I liked challenges. Mathematics was very different to learn than other disciplines. Learning mathematics required the teacher to give the student time to process the information more than other disciplines because it takes the brain more time to assimilate the information. This varies, of course, with the student's ability and the level of difficulty of the mathematics course.

I entered each class with enthusiasm, energy, praise, and humor. I always kept in mind that no mathematics textbook is perfect in its development of topics. I wrote my presentations to my classes on the chalkboard or whiteboard. Students were required to take notes, and the lessons they learned were then incorporated into their homework. As I developed a topic on the chalkboard, I stopped intermittently and posed questions to students, making sure they understood what I was saying. Oftentimes, I'd stop what I was doing and simply ask, "Why?" Most students were eager to answer my questions, and different students were called upon each time.

Next, I had a related sample problem using the same questioning technique with the students. This approach kept the students active and participating in the learning process. Other topics were presented in the same way. I considered rote memorization to be a mode of brain function that lead to little retention. After homework assignments were given, I usually circulated around the classroom to help my students or answer lingering questions.

I was always a firm believer that it is extremely important to give students words of encouragement and praiseworthy responses. Students of mathematics must know their teacher cares about their learning mathematics. One doesn't learn mathematics instantly, and the teacher must encourage patience and tenacity to be a part of the student's learning curve. However, when the students were just visiting with each other, I sometimes eavesdropped and then delivered humorous little vignettes for which they could only laugh at. My ability to provide these vignettes from time to time amazed me at first. Other humor included random jokes, such as "What kind of undergarment does a mermaid wear? An algae bra!" or "What form of math promotes plant growth? Gee, I'm a tree!"

Maintaining discipline within the classroom was never difficult because I am five feet ten inches tall, full-figured, and I have a loud, resonant voice. These three characteristics were used effectively. I had one student who was procrastinating too frequently. One day, I thought of the right thing to say to Kevin. I firmly told him, "Kevin, it's not liking you that is the problem, but liking the manner in which you conduct yourself." Kevin asked me math-related questions after that, did his homework on time, and eventually improved his test scores.

Andrea was a student in pre-calculus. On the last day of school, she asked me to laugh all period long because she didn't want to forget what my laughter sounded like. It was a sweet compliment. One last day in my advanced math class, a semester of matrix algebra, and a semester of probability and statistics, my twelve students presented me with a dozen red roses. Each rose had a private message attached to a stem. Tears welled in my eyes, and I was almost speechless at the kind gesture. Later in the day, I made sure the administrators saw the roses!

At the end of the school year, in all my classes, I treated my students to singing the German folk song, "Du, du liegst mir im Herzen," which translates into "You, you are in my heart." Some classrooms with sliding walls opened their walls just so they could hear the song, too.

As I mentioned earlier, I avoided teaching by rote memorization at all costs. Students who used practiced rote memorization so often didn't remember a thing they learned. Developing critical thinking skills from the start is the key to success. Since the brain can only process so much information, I had to manage the balance between boredom and burnout to maintain my students' interest in mathematics.

My questioning techniques stimulated student ownership of topics while encouraging critical thinking. If the students formulated solutions in their own words, they'd ultimately feel more engaged in the learning process as a whole.

Being a person who is conscious of her own state of mind, I gained empathy with the state of mind of my students. In an ironic way, I may actually have benefited from my own bipolar disorder—at least with having to manage it and be aware of it. I knew what depression was, and I knew that frustration could trigger it in a person. I also knew that overcoming frustrations helped me avoid depression and made me feel better. I was sensitive to this in my students and helped them avoid feelings of depression.

Mathematics was not the easiest subject for me, but I accepted the challenge of mastering it. The challenge came from stories told by my mother about my grandfather, Paustian, who never formalized his mathematics skill but was legendary in his problem-solving skills. He died before I was born but, through my mother, his life had a great impact on me. I was not as motivated to be a housewife as my fellow female relatives. Somehow, overcoming the challenge of understanding math fulfilled me. I never felt doing math provoked an episode of bipolar disorder, but a bipolar episode could preclude solving a math problem. I believe that mastering mathematics had something to do with my ability to manage my own bipolar disorder.

I delighted in tutoring others and sharing my skills with people. Helping others meet the challenge of mathematics helped me fight my depression. Sharing my skills as a mathematician brought me satisfaction, similar to overcoming the challenge of mathematics itself. I sought both doing and sharing mathematics as a way to fulfill my needs and keep my depression at bay. I was never quite sure whether I fought depression so I could do and share mathematics, or if I used teaching mathematics as a way to fight off the depression.

As I pursued my career as a mathematics teacher, I also began to focus on three topics—children, marriage, and career—and whether or not I could manage all three at the same time. I started asking myself questions: *Should a woman with bipolar disorder have children? Would her children have the problems I have? Should I burden them with that potential genetic problem? Could I find a spouse who could tolerate my bipolar disorder? Would it be possible to manage my condition with a companion, or would that complicate things too much? Could I pursue a career teaching mathematics while managing my bipolar condition? Could I get the necessary medical help while keeping my condition under control and concealed from the workplace?* In retrospect, I considered each of those questions for a long time as I continued to make life-forming decisions.

Another fulfilling experience for me was the collegiality of teacher institutes. I participated in many of these as part of my professional development. After Sputnick in 1959, the National Science Foundation sponsored institutes for high school teachers of mathematics and the sciences to improve their skills relative to similar teachers in the Soviet Union. As the recipient of four National Science Foundation institutes, I felt a moral obligation to make a contribution to American society. In the year I was born, no other country would have given me the opportunities that America did. God Bless America!

Part of the training in the institutes involved preparing students for their exams and challenging them with a high level of problem-solving. To that end, I gave multipart exams. Every exam had some multiple-choice questions and some workout problems. Correcting the exams was not my favorite activity, but it goes with the territory. Just marking them wrong was of little service to the student. Instead, I circled the mistake in red and wrote in the correct line of work. This took time but was worth it.

On the evening before a pre-calculus or AP calculus exam, I held a review session at the high school at seven o'clock at night. Many students showed up. Leading the students through the review was not my strategy. Instead, I made students ask questions on what they specifically wanted to review because it made them think about particular topics before asking questions.

Many students came back to see me after a year's college study to let me know how well they were prepared to study mathematics in college. Additional follow-up graduation surveys at the high school mentioned my name frequently with regard to teachers who had prepared students well.

In the summer of 1972, I accepted a two-week National Science Foundation Summer Institute at Northern Arizona University in Flagstaff, Arizona. At the institute, topics of discrete mathematics, or finite mathematics, were studied. Some of these topics included matrix algebra, mathematical induction, probability, and combinatorics.

While I was in Arizona, I took a trip to the Grand Canyon. As I stood on the South Rim, I was totally in awe of what I saw. Of all the places I have seen in the world, I didn't know there was a place left that could knock my socks off with its sheer pristine beauty. Now I know why the Grand Canyon is one of the seven natural wonders of the world!

On the journey back to Iowa, I stopped in Albuquerque, New Mexico, to visit my cousin, Dr. Henry Stuart Schuldt, who worked in the Sandia Corporation there. Hank graduated from the University of Iowa with a PhD in physical chemistry. In jest, he said he liked his job so well that he didn't need to be paid! Hank and I had a wonderful visit. I'm glad I visited him when I did. He passed away in 1991 at the age of sixty-two.

In 1976, my cousin, Klaus, also made a trek to the United States. When I picked him up at the airport, I drove by Blackhawk State Park. Sure enough, there was an Indian pow-wow in session. With his camera, Klaus got as many pictures as possible at dusk. He was amazed that this type of pow-wow even existed in the United States anymore. He stayed at Aunt Annie's home with her husband, Henry, while he was in town.

The Bettendorf High School administration welcomed Klaus graciously. I remember how he commented on the school's swimming pool. "No wonder so many Americans win the gold medal in swimming in the Olympics," he said. Klaus had read a lot about Abraham Lincoln and his life, and he was captivated by the late president. One weekend, we journeyed to Springfield, Illinois, on a Friday night after school. What we found in Springfield was a huge Kaaba Shrine parade. Naturally, Klaus pulled out his camera and took many pictures. When it was time to find a place to stay for the night, we couldn't find one! Finally, one motel room became available. I suggested we share it, but Klaus wanted no part of that! Finally, we found two different motel rooms and rested for the evening.

Saturday was devoted entirely to Abraham Lincoln. We visited the Lincoln Memorial and even rubbed Lincoln's nose. We went inside Lincoln's former home and the Illinois state capitol building. "The architecture was very clumsy," Klaus noted.

New Salem State Park was the highlight of the day. We noticed that earphones were available as we approached each building, but they were only in English. Klaus was given a long sheet of paper typed on both sides in German. What I heard in my earphones, I translated into German as best as I could. The spirit of Lincoln is certainly in New Salem when you see his law offices.

We spent Sunday touring the Mormon settlement in the Nauvoo, Illinois, area. On the Illinois side of the Mississippi River, opposite Burlington, Iowa, there was a beautiful river drive with abundant autumn leaves that Klaus and I really enjoyed. At dinnertime, we dined at the Hotel Nauvoo. We tried the local wine and bleu cheese. The meat entrees were fried catfish and a ham selection. Potatoes and vegetables were standard fare. Klaus said this was the best meal he had ever had in America. I was pleased that I could enjoy this journey with him. Shortly after his return to Germany, when he was in his late thirties or early forties, he, too, needed to be hospitalized for bipolar disorder, which his mother had also had. Then, at the age of forty-six, Klaus passed away because of kidney cancer in both of his kidneys. Klaus's father also died of kidney cancer at the age of seventy-five. The hand of fate is sometimes very difficult in the Stuhr family.

Speaking of ill fate, I had a few medical problems while at Bettendorf High School. Earlier, I referred to my ruptured appendix. Three weeks after my father's death in 1975, I smashed my left elbow by falling on slippery ice while going to get my hair done. I called my friend, Ronna, and she quickly took me to the hospital emergency room. The orthopedic surgeon said I had two choices: surgery or never being able to use my arm again. *Some choices!* I thought sarcastically. The surgery was successful and my elbow is now as good as new. In 1996, I was diagnosed with breast cancer and underwent a lumpectomy. In 2006, after my retirement, pre-cancerous polyps and immense fibrous tissue were found in my uterus, even though I had a D and C previously. A hysterectomy was in order, and I felt much better after it was over.

There were humorous times in the Math Department at Bettendorf High School. One math teacher, Manatee, was infamous for answering the third-floor telephone. He'd say, "Third-floor laundry?" However, it wasn't so funny when the superintendent had called and received that greeting. Another funny incident occurred one Monday morning as I reported to work. The school secretarial staff was buzzing with excitement over my engagement.

Apparently, there were two women named Joann Stuhr in the area. The other Joann Stuhr announced her engagement in the Sunday newspaper without showing her picture. I found the situation comical and, at lunchtime, I nonchalantly switched my pearl ring from my right hand to my left hand before going into the main office. Everybody was showering me with congratulatory comments. When I showed them my ring, the women in the room grew even giddier. They wanted to know when a good date for a shower would be. At that point, I couldn't control my laughter any longer. I told them the real story. As I left, I overheard someone say, "Better luck next time."

After the basketball season was over, there was a traditional B-Club fundraising event in the old high school gymnasium. In March of 1972, this event consisted of two teams of high school players, chosen by the coaches, to play each other in a full-court exhibition basketball game. There always was a faculty member in costume to promote this event. The weekly announcements promoted the appearance of the famous "Annie Oakley" at the game. Wearing my father's bib overalls and his red and blue plaid flannel shirt, I began dressing to appear like Annie Oakley. A red scarf adorned my neck in a circular fashion and was anchored in place. My hair was very long, falling halfway down the middle of my back. My hair was French-braided into two long, thick pigtails, secured with rubber bands and adorned with red bows, like one would place on a gift package.

Upon entering the gymnasium, I joined the two teams in tossing the basketballs around. When I dribbled the basketball around, the students easily stole it from me. That was all right by me because it made it fun for them. At halftime, I went in front of the girls' locker room to meet my dad. He had a box with some straw in it that contained a week-old male baby pig. I cradled the baby pig against my body with my right arm and returned to the gymnasium. As soon as the students saw the piglet, pandemonium broke out.

Students gave the sight of Annie Oakley with her baby pig a standing ovation. All I could hear was laughter, applause, whistles of all kinds, and tons of screaming. As I circled the gymnasium floor in order to have the students see the pig better, I carefully lifted it up with both hands. Unfortunately, I scared the pig and he peed on me! The second the students realized he had peed on me, they went totally and irrevocably ballistic. Administrators were also present and saw that I was a good sport. Returning the baby pig to my father, I told him what a huge spectacle the whole thing had been. Dad laughed and later returned the baby pig to its mother.

That day, it dawned on me that I had enough of an actress in me to pull off anything if I really wanted to! I had enough of a farm girl spirit in me to pull the pig close to me even after it had done its deed. This episode further endeared me to my students. In retrospect, I never did anything that compromised my ability to teach my students; I only did things to enhance my relationship with them.

In 1974, we had individualized instructions with a computer-based plan from the Westinghouse Corporation. This plan had mixed results and was abandoned soon after its implementation. During that time, the students in my math analysis class were falling behind in their work.

My Fair Lady was on television at the time. The next day, I wrote a large message on the board for my math analysis students. On the board was: LIKE ELIZA DOOLITTLE SAID AT THE ASCOT RACE, "GET OFF YOUR BLOOMING _ _ _ AND MAKE SOME REAL PROGRESS!" Soon after, I received a typewritten note to go to the principal's office. I was worried my quote had been met with some disapproval. I soon left for the principal's office when Ivan, another math teacher, stopped me in the hall. The note was a prank! *Whew, what a relief!* I thought. Apparently, I wasn't the only one in the Math Department with a sense of humor.

At Bettendorf High School, as with other schools, we often had all-school assemblies in the gymnasium. One year, for homecoming, we had a faculty skit with Franc, one of the male teachers, and his "harem." The tallest and largest women faculty members dressed up in togas and danced, pranced, and jumped around the gymnasium to "attract" Franc. Once I jumped so high, I accidentally pulled my toga up a little too high. I was careful not to jump so high after that; I didn't want to end up standing there in my slip on the gymnasium floor! I was relieved when the finale came without incident. Students always reacted well to my participation in these humorous events. They went so far as to pressure other teachers to do the same.

In the fall of 1973, Bettendorf High School opened in its new facility on Eighteenth Street. Prior to that, Bettendorf High School functioned in three different buildings. One building was the old senior high school gymnasium complex. A second building was the old junior high school adjacent to the old senior high school complex. The third building was a rented insurance building down the Twenty-First Street hill to the "flatland" near the Mississippi River in downtown Bettendorf. Biology and social studies were taught in this building. Students named the building the "wildlife" building. Students coming from that particular building were often late, giving other students time to study or time to horse around while they were waiting.

One day, I heard a scuffle in the hallway. As I turned the corner to find out what the commotion was, one of my students, John O'Connell, had already released a huge snowball, which hit me squarely in the abdomen. My immediate reaction was to laugh. I understood my students when they were left to themselves, and I knew they often acted up while they waited for order to take over again. John and Jeff Ingleby, another student of mine, had been throwing snowballs in the hallway. They immediately apologized profusely—especially after John realized what he had done—and cleaned up the slippery mess. I didn't need to give them any instructions; they knew they were out of line. And because we had an understanding, I saw no further need for disciplinary action.

Iowa law required that Bettendorf High School have two fire drills and two tornado drills in the course of a school year. The buzzers for the fire and tornado drills were very similar in tone. One day, a buzzer sounded. Half of the staff members and students went outside the building, thinking it was the fire drill; the other half of the staff members and students stayed inside the building because it was actually a tornado drill. I became the laughing stock of the school, being one of the teachers who took her students outside during a tornado drill. My students jokingly chastised me for taking them into the teeth of a tornado! Subsequent to this drill, it was announced over the public address system whether it was fire drill or a tornado drill before the buzzer sounded.

I was always happy when I could be a clown or an actress at the school. Displaying anger or being in an argument led my brain to feel like it was going back and forth, making me feel disoriented. I learned to avoid confrontation by changing the subject, making a trip to the restroom, taking a walk outside, or figuring out some other way to distract myself. Once in a while, I could clear my head of anger and think of something cheerful to stay out of an argument. I never had those feelings of disorientation or depression when I was clowning around, even in front of the entire student body in an assembly.

Skipping my medications led to feelings of sluggishness that could lead to confrontations with others who didn't understand my situation. This made it all the more difficult to keep my bipolar condition a secret. I suppose, in a way, I was an actress all the time; I tried hard to keep a poker face and smile all the time. I felt pretty sneaky by purchasing my drugs across town, and I felt crafty by paying my own medical bills so that no one in the school would know I was bipolar. I could maintain a poker face and still be all eyes and ears.

Teaching during the 1970s was a time of many incidents that brought out my sense of humor. I was always careful to use these incidents to endear myself to my students and allow them to feel comfortable learning math from someone who shared their youthful enthusiasm. I was slightly concerned that my administrators would judge some of the incidents as inappropriate; however, I never received any formal criticism for them. One day in 1980, I had occasion to be in the main office where Principal Robert E. Owen and Assistant Principal John T. Kelly were behind the counter. Principal Owen was known for his good sense of character and hired good teachers; Assistant Principal Kelly was known for his discipline and attention to detail. We had a very pleasant conversation. They left me with their thoughts that I had plenty of drive and ambition. Their words encouraged me and built up my self-confidence. I respected these two leaders and was pleased to hear them encourage me to keep doing what I was doing.

I was diagnosed with breast cancer in the summer of 1996. On August 6, a lumpectomy was performed on my right breast in the outpatient lab of a local hospital. The tumor was cancerous but small—nine millimeters in length. A week later, the lymph node dissection was performed under my right arm. The doctors wanted me to report to the hospital the night before because the lymph node dissection was to be performed very early the next morning. I called my sister Madeleine, who lived ninety miles away, asking her to take me to the hospital. Mostly, I was looking for moral support. She said she couldn't do that.

I drove my car to the hospital the night before and left it in the hospital parking lot. My sister and brother-in-law came to the hospital the next morning at ten o'clock to take me home. We looked at my niece's wedding pictures at my apartment. They left shortly thereafter because they noticed that my anesthetics still left me a bit groggy. Luckily, there was no cancer in my lymph nodes.

Before my lumpectomy, I had evicted the tenants from the red brick farmhouse because of late rental payments and, after a year's warning, not mowing the grass, which was now close to a foot tall. This farmhouse, on its acreage, was the homestead Madeleine and I had inherited from our parents. From the outset, my sister wanted to sell the farmhouse and acreage, but I didn't want to. Besides, I had managed it for the five years my mother didn't live there prior to her passing. Throughout the years, my sister and brother-in-law came down to help me clean the farmhouse between tenants. Gradually, my sister tired of cleaning the farmhouse, saying she didn't want to clean up other people's messes. My perspective was that renting a farmhouse was a business that required a certain amount of responsibility just like any other business.

After the lymph node dissection, I had all I could do to prepare lesson plans for a new scheduling system at the high school. While I healed, I was absent from school for the first few weeks. During that time, I had to prepare lessons for a substitute teacher, which is often more time-consuming than being there. This was particularly true since the new scheduling system had us meeting twice as long each day but only meeting half a year for a year-long course. This was referred to as "block scheduling." It was particularly tricky when teaching mathematics. Not being there and trying to schedule classes for a substitute teacher was very stressful on me.

My sister called me in mid-September to ask how I was doing. "Fine," I said, but I was lying through my teeth. I didn't have to go through chemotherapy; however, I did endure thirty-five radiation treatments that began on September 29, 1996. I asked my radiation oncologist if I could start cleaning the farmhouse. He said that cleaning would be fine; my body would tell me when it was tired. Before each radiation treatment when I arrived at the hospital, I sang songs and told jokes just to keep my spirits up. When under radiation, I imagined a dartboard on the ceiling named Madeleine. I threw imaginary darts at the dartboard because I knew my sister wasn't going to help me clean the farmhouse. *Where is my sister's compassion? Where is her responsibility?* I wondered.

I didn't want to have to deal with a large vacant red brick farmhouse with a furnace that needed to be checked periodically in the winter by myself. Locks constantly had to be rekeyed on the outside doors of the farmhouse. Twenty-two storm windows with eight panes each needed to be cleaned. The carpets were dirty and enhanced by the smell of a Great Dane—one that had been kept in the basement by previous tenants, contrary to their lease agreement. The carpet going upstairs had so many holes in it that it was unsafe to walk on anymore.

But those were all things that needed taking care of. I had new carpet and padding installed in the living room, dining room, sun porch, and on the stairs leading to the second floor, as well as in the entryway to the rooms on the second floor. Kitchen carpet was installed in the kitchen. Both bathrooms were cleaned, including the rust from the combination shower and bathtub. The coat hanging area was also remodeled. One Saturday, I spent the entire day cleaning and waxing the oak floors of the three bedrooms. They had been filthy with cigarette butts, but I was able to get them sparkling like new again with a good floor cleaner.

As I arduously cleaned the floor and tried not to focus on resenting my sister too much, I kept thinking, *You'll never get the best of me.* While I took time to scrub and renovate the farmhouse, I was also working full-time at Bettendorf High School. On top of that, I was trying to take care of my health. My sister, on the other hand, was not working outside of her home.

Two new tenants moved in on Thanksgiving Day in 1996. They were the best tenants we had ever had. They knew the value of good land and the work it takes to keep it up. They respected the place in which they lived, and I really respected them for that. Several years later, the county assessor listed the assessed value of the red brick farmhouse at $100,000—a sizeable increase over the last assessment.

In mid-December of that year, my sister called me to ask for a key to the farmhouse. I told her she couldn't go there; there were new tenants in the farmhouse. She asked how long they had been there, and I told her they had moved in on Thanksgiving Day. She didn't have anything else to say to me, and so we hung up the phone. A few months later, she had asked where her share of the rent was. I had to tell her I was withholding the money I spent to fix the house. She had no idea what had to be done to get it in shape to rent again. I was very disappointed with my sister's lack of responsibility.

When my lumpectomy healed, I was ready for seven weeks of radiation treatment, Monday through Friday. I had the school's permission to leave every day to meet my afternoon appointment at three thirty. One day, Brandon, an associate principal, asked me to come to his office after school. I showed up in his office a little after three o'clock in the afternoon for our meeting. I learned that he wanted me to sign up for an AEA course so that I could become a better teacher. I said okay and slowly stood up to walk out of his office. He said he was just trying to be a good coach and wanted to talk about the opportunity some more. It was well after three thirty when I finally admitted that I was late for my radiation appointment. When I left his office, I was crying, but the school's secretary was still there. She said that the administration didn't know what it was doing. She helped me call the cancer center and arrange a late radiation treatment. I could not believe how insensitive Brandon was.

Finally, I went and got my treatment, even though I ended up missing my original appointment. The next morning, I made an appointment to finish the conference in the associate principal's office. Oddly, he never followed up with me about the training opportunity again.

All circumstances considered, I've said it before and I'll say it again: My years of teaching at Bettendorf High School were the most satisfying years in my career.

Chapter 12:

Hiding My Condition

I was aware that two of my father's siblings had been diagnosed with bipolar disorder. Aunt Ria was confined to a mental hospital in Germany for fifteen years because doctors were unable to find the correct treatment for her. Many times, her son, Klaus, would come home from school and never knew where his mother was. Uncle Ernst, who later joined my father in America, suffered from frequent periods of depression. With these periods of depression, Dad would work with Uncle Ernst in cleaning the cattle barns and hog barns. They also worked together to grind feed for the cattle and hogs.

In talking to Uncle Ernst when he was having bad days, Dad would always try to turn his brother's head around to focus on another perspective. These incidents occurred more when winter became springtime. Dad's nature was always to help his brother during these trying times. But there were times when Dad became frustrated, too. One time, he came home from a long day of working, washed his hands in the kitchen sink, and muttered, "If I'd have known it was going to be like this, my brother could have stayed in Germany!"

Despite getting annoyed sometimes, Dad usually kept his feelings bottled up inside. My family knew that he was the best keeper his brother ever had. Sadly, when Dad passed away, the support for Uncle Ernst was no longer there. About a year after Dad's passing, Uncle Ernst shot and killed his wife and then took his own life. The irony of his death is that he never sought medical help.

I was very, *very* fortunate that I met Dr. Sidecar some nine months before my employment began at Bettendorf High School. He placed me on prescription drugs after my first appointment with him. He monitored the situation closely and sometimes made slight prescription changes for me until it was perfect for me. I was on Eskalith, Prozac, and Dalmane for most of the time that I worked at Bettendorf High School. Not once did I have a manic episode while I taught there. Dr. Sidecar was a godsend. Literally, he saved my whole academic career. And after my hysterectomy in 2005, Dr. Sidecar changed most of my medications again. He hit the nail on the head; I've never felt so good as I do today.

As I mentioned before, my doctor originally thought my condition was depression. Only later did he refer to it as bipolar disorder. He explained to me that bipolar disorder is a chemical imbalance in the brain. It is also hereditary. While there is treatment for bipolar disorder, there is no cure. It is neither a character flaw nor a personality defect. Many people are in denial of having bipolar disorder because they don't know how it will affect them in the future. This was the same of me; I tried to deny all of the earlier signals.

Insomnia has the ability to trigger bipolar disorder. I denied that insomnia affected my brain's function for years. However, I was lucky that there were people around who could help me whenever an incident came on. Not everyone is that lucky. One place to look for help is a local mental health center. Psychiatrists can be assigned to find the correct medicine to restore the chemical balance in the brain. If you or someone you know lives with bipolar disorder, remember that you have options. If you are unsatisfied with your current doctor, simply find another psychiatrist who can work with you to find the correct medicines.

Besides the insomnia, I also noticed that anger made my brain have occasional shooting pains. If I gave into ridicule, I would feel pain in my head. If I simply ignored ridicule, the pain would not come. A strong temper runs in my family; I was ridiculed often. Dealing with this was a challenge for me, especially when I was growing up.

When I started employment at Bettendorf High School, I decided to heed my father's advice and keep my bipolar disorder a secret. Quite frankly, there was no one I could trust. My health insurance was used only for my smashed left elbow; I paid for my psychiatrist's appointments myself. I also paid for my prescription drugs myself at a pharmacy way on the west end of Davenport so that nobody would recognize me. There was no legislation to protect me. There was no disability act to protect me. I had to be as sneaky and crafty as I could be to protect myself.

I worked long hours from Monday through Thursday. On top of that, I still had tests to correct and new tests to compose when I got home. I kept pushing myself to do a good job, and I seldom went to bed before midnight. When Friday rolled around, I was always really tired. The routine on Fridays after school became one of undressing and going to bed. Around ten o'clock at night, I'd awake to go to the bathroom and take my evening medications. Then I'd go back to bed and sleep until eight o'clock the next morning. I always felt refreshed on the weekends.

The former official name for bipolar disorder—manic-depressive illness—is still in frequent use today. According to the *APA Dictionary of Psychology,* bipolar disorders are a group of mood disorders in which both manic and depressive symptoms occur. Depressive disorder is any one of the mood disorders that typically have sadness as one of their symptoms. Manic episode is characterized by elevative, expansive, or irritable moods with three or more of the following symptoms: an increase in activity, talkativeness, racing thoughts, inflated self-esteem, a decreased need for sleep, extreme distractibility, and involvement in pleasurable activities that are likely to have unfortunate consequences, such as buying sprees, foolish investments, sexual indiscretions, or reckless driving. All of these symptoms impair normal functioning and relationships with others.

I currently take five prescription drugs at bedtime each night. One of the drugs is for an inactive thyroid, and the other one is a sleeping pill. As I mentioned, bipolar disorder can be triggered by a lack of sleep, or insomnia. I could generally tell when I didn't get enough sleep; I was more sluggish in the morning and somewhat lethargic in my thinking. As the day progressed, I became aware of how much better I functioned. I knew from this that I needed to take some time and get some extra sleep. As I became older, the symptoms of bipolar disorder became more apparent. However, by that time I had effective routines that were in place.

People have often asked me why I didn't get married. Simply put, I always knew that I wouldn't be able to manage it all: have a fulfilling marriage, bear children, and have a successful career. Had I done so, I would have made a mess of all three. It would have been too stressful for me, and stress is incompatible with bipolar disorder. In the end, I decided it just wasn't worth it to try and pursue all three.

Chapter 13:

Publishing and Awards

As I got closer to retirement, various awards for my years as an educator started coming my way. Happy Joe Whitty established a teacher recognition program for fifty thousand Scott County teachers. In 1989, I received the Golden Apple Award in the second group of twenty-five teachers chosen. My mother was still alive to see me receive the award.

In 1991, 1992, and 1995, I received Iowa's Presidential Award for Excellence in the Teaching of Mathematics. Three secondary mathematics teachers are chosen each year to receive the award. A national winner from the three candidates is chosen in Washington, D.C. Meanwhile, in Iowa, there were recognition ceremonies in Governor Branstad's office in the state capitol, as well as at the Iowa Council of Teachers of Mathematics Convention. While no other math teachers congratulated me for this achievement, many science teachers and other teachers at Bettendorf High School congratulated me on the state awards. These awards will always be cherished dearly.

I wrote four articles that were published in the Iowa Council of Teachers of Mathematics Journal. The articles were on graph theory, the Fibonacci sequence, matrix algebra, and the complete approach on mathematical induction. One of my former students at Bettendorf High School, Tina Ruwe, matriculated at Northwestern University in Evanston, Illinois. When she went back to Bettendorf to see me, she told me that her mathematics professor at Northwestern University knew of me through the articles I had published in the *Iowa Council of Teachers of Mathematics Journal.* Furthermore, eight presentations were made by yours truly at state, regional, and national conferences of teachers of mathematics.

These were all wonderful experiences. I was asked so many challenging and intelligent questions. The majority of my presentations were on graphing calculators; newer models were being introduced every year, teachers were curious about their capabilities. My gratitude goes out to Bettendorf High School for providing a place that I could grow and flourish.

When I considered getting a PhD, I recalled a conversation with Mary Ann, my teacher friend from my Okinawa days. She had earned her PhD with an emphasis on shorthand writing and was teaching at Morehead State College in Kentucky. When I asked her what she missed from high school teaching, she admitted that she couldn't show her personality as much in college. That's when I decided not to earn my PhD. I knew that I needed to show my personality in the high school classroom to keep myself happy.

Chapter 14:

Death of My Parents

Several years after I started teaching at Bettendorf High School, my father passed away from colon and liver cancer in 1975. When my mother, my sister, my brother-in-law, my niece, my nephew, and I walked into his hospital room, Dad shook hands with everybody but me. After that, I'd always stop at the hospital on my way home from school to talk with him one-on-one. In the evening, I'd pick up Mom and bring her to Dad's hospital room. One evening, however, I had a very difficult assignment.

Dad had recently deposited $12,000 in the bank. The bank officials told us to have Dad sign a withdrawal slip for the corn. When I asked him to sign the blue piece of paper, he was very confused. He had not heard the doctor tell him that afternoon that he was dying because he had not been wearing his hearing aids. I quickly left his room and walked down the hall to get a big gulp of water. Returning to the room, I held Dad's hand and reminded him of all the things that he had done right.

Dad was always very proud of how well he did in school. He said that every day of school was important; there was no excuse for staying home and doing the work there. He was especially proud that he instilled a strong work ethic in me as well. His one regret was that he didn't take piano lessons in Germany, and he was insistent that Madeleine and I take them. Dad was also insistent that Madeleine and I be baptized and confirmed at Trinity Lutheran Church in Davenport, Iowa. What a gift! Even today, it brings tears to my eyes to know that he brought his daughters to the Lord. I couldn't bring myself to talk about the bad things in my father's life;

what would be the point of it? When I was done talking and comforting Dad, he quietly signed the withdrawal slip.

On our way home, Mom asked me how I could bring myself to say what I said to Dad. "The words were just there," I said. I knew that I was the most emotional one in my family. Later, when I told Dr. Sidecar the story with Dad, he told me that I had done a great job. However, with bipolar disorder, sometimes I spoke words that did not make any sense. Dr. Sidecar adjusted my medication slightly and instructed me not to talk to anybody nor go to school to teach for a week so that I could properly mourn and get my thoughts in order.

After my father passed away, Mom continued living in the red brick farmhouse by herself. I began helping her with everyday things. I took her to her doctor's appointments and prepared TV dinners with either roast beef or roast turkey, mashed potatoes, and a favorite vegetable. She could then simply heat these TV dinners in her toaster oven, especially on days when she wasn't feeling so well. We conversed by telephone every day, and even set up a little system where she would recite her grocery list to me over the phone. Afterwards, I would pick up the groceries for her. I even hired high school students who would mow the grass on the premises.

During this time, Mom really became more than my mother; she became my friend. Frequently, she said to me, "I can count on you, Joann." She talked about all aspects of her life that I never knew before. In short, she told me how her whole life had been. We agreed that it is the quality of our relationships that sustains us against all adversity.

When I called my mother in early April 1986, I remember her voice being so weak. She said she didn't feel well. As soon as we hung up the phone, I headed to the red brick farmhouse. Mom had so many layers of clothes on, and yet she was still freezing. Her breathing was shallow, too. I immediately called her doctor, and he told me to bring her to the hospital as soon as possible. She was in the hospital for a week with pneumonia.

When my mother was finally released from the hospital, I paid for a caregiver service so that one of several ladies would be with her from nine o'clock in the morning until five o'clock in the afternoon Monday through Friday. This arrangement worked quite well. One day, the woman who went to the house had forgotten her lunch. She took one of Mom's TV dinners without first asking. This didn't please my mother very well, but it indicated to me she was beginning to feel better!

On May 19, 1986, my mother celebrated her eighty-sixth birthday. That July, she was able to be by herself again without a caregiver present. She loved to be outdoors, tend to her flowers, and pull out weeds from the flowerbeds. Since the red brick farmhouse was so close to Interstate-80, she always locked the doors when she was both in the farmhouse and when she was outdoors. Locking the doors made her feel safer.

August 24, 1986, was a very warm summer day with accompanying high humidity. Mom went into the farmhouse around one o'clock in the afternoon. She made sure the house doors were locked before she took a nap. At around three o'clock in the afternoon, two teenaged males knocked at the south door, wanting some water. She brought paper cups to the ledge on the south porch and quickly locked the door behind her again. There were water faucets on the outside of the house. She went back to napping.

About an hour later, she heard another knock at the south door. The same two teenagers wanted to borrow her telephone book. She was groggy, having been awakened from a deep sleep, and she wasn't thinking. As she opened the door to hand the telephone book to the teens, they pushed through the door, wanting her car. One of them grabbed her arm and held it tightly. She looked at them incredulously and asked, "You wouldn't hurt an old lady, would you?"

"Not if you do what we tell you to do!" they responded coldly.

Mom walked to the kitchen with her arms against the walls, pretending she was having difficulty walking. She then opened the closet door and pointed to her purse, which contained her car keys. The older teenager took the purse and immediately went over to the dining room table. The younger teen instructed my mother to go sit on a stool by the south door. He then went to the kitchen to cut the telephone cable. Mom did as she was told. However, when she turned around to see what the older teenager was doing at the dining room table, the younger one immediately told her to sit still or he would shoot her.

The older teenager found my mother's car keys and also removed her money from her billfold. As soon as the teens left the house, Mom immediately locked the south screen door and the south wooden door. She checked to see if the electricity was on for the garage door opener—and it was. The switch was turned to the OFF position. The culprits didn't know enough to use the ripcord to open the garage door. Instead, they backed my mother's car through the garage door.

My mother contemplated what to do next. She decided to walk one-half mile to the neighbor's house. Leaving the house with her purse, heart medicine, and a few other valuables, she took her time walking through the orchard and cornfield. She counted in six rows from the gravel road so that she wouldn't get lost. Then she came to a fence before the next cornfield. This fence had a wooden post that my limber mother climbed quite easily. She used six rows of corn near the gravel road as her marker before going through the second cornfield. Then she came across a herd of cows surrounded by an electric fence that was twelve inches from the ground. Knowing she would get an electric shock if she stepped over the fence, she slid her body under the fence. When she stood up, her neighbor, George A. Maxwell, saw her and hurried to her rescue. After she explained what had happened, George called the Scott County sheriff's office to report the burglary.

While all of that was going on, I had been busy developing the curriculum for a new advanced placement calculus course at Bettendorf High School. When I got home, I noticed that there was a message on my answering machine from George's wife, Alice, briefly explaining what had happened. I immediately called her back to get the details, and then I drove straight to my mother's farmhouse. Mom wasn't distraught, nor was she trembling when I showed up. However, she wanted to stay in George and Alice's home that night.

I returned to Bettendorf High School to gather curriculum materials because I knew I would be spending the rest of the summer vacation with my mother. When I went back to the farmhouse, Mom told me different parts of the burglary. With her information, I prepared a report for the Scott County sheriff's office so that my mother wouldn't have to testify. The sheriff's office kept us informed about the two burglars. The older teenager had a prison record. The younger one was a runaway from a juvenile home, and his father was a prison warden in Illinois. The two burglars had abandoned a stolen pickup truck on Interstate-80 near LeClaire, Iowa. Then they walked westward along Interstate-80, looking for another vehicle to steal. Husky farmer Meier proved to be an obstacle for them, even though he had a pickup truck in the barnyard with the keys in the ignition and a billfold on the seat with money in it. Their next target was my mother's place.

Trooper Todd of the Indiana State Police arrested them on the interstate well east of Indianapolis. They were incarcerated in Indiana. About a week or so later, I received a telephone call from a Scott County sheriff's deputy. Two county deputies were going to Indiana to bring the incarcerated back to Scott County Jail so they could be prosecuted. They wanted to know if I wanted to make the trip to Indiana so that I could drive my mother's car back to Iowa. I told them I would.

The journey to Indiana was in a paddy wagon. Along the way, I found myself chuckling silently that I was riding in a paddy wagon. The sheriff's deputies were good conversationalists. When we arrived at the Indiana jail where the two criminals were incarcerated, the two deputies asked me to read Trooper Todd's report. Trooper Todd said one of the two arrested was a real bastard. The two deputies took me to my mother's car. They helped me clean up the backseat, which contained empty soda bottles, pretzels, potato chips, and lots of soiled underwear. I thanked the deputies and was soon on my way back to Iowa in Mom's car.

Later, Mom revealed to me that she had promised Dad on his deathbed that she would continue to live in the red brick farmhouse. However, Dad would never have wanted her to live in the farmhouse alone if she didn't feel safe there. Mom and I decided that a condominium would be a better living situation for her. We began looking at different condos. Finally, we found one in Walcott, Iowa.

Mom made a down payment, and a bunch of us moved her in on the Friday after Thanksgiving. Imagine making the move from a fifty-year stay in a farmhouse to a condominium! Lee and Martha Polley, Alice's sister, helped us immensely. We filled boxes upon boxes and loaded them into cars. We also carefully put china and dishes into large plastic buckets. Once all of the vehicles were completely filled, we'd drive over to the new condo and unload everything. We drove back and forth numerous times. The items were then placed in Mom's condo, and she would tell us where she wanted everything to go. Mom and I could never have moved everything on our own. I am eternally grateful to Lee and Martha for helping us. At the end of the day, all that was left were the large and heavy items.

On Thanksgiving Day, I visited my mother at her condo. I brought two roasted turkey drumsticks for us to eat together. We attended to the final details of her move during the afternoon. In the evening, I assisted Mom with getting in and out of the bathtub. I also washed her hair—which was getting more difficult for her to do herself—and helped her pin-curl her hair. When I left that night, I grinned and said, "Happy Thanksgiving, Mom!" She just laughed.

The following Friday after Thanksgiving, I had driven a U-Haul truck to the farmhouse around nine o'clock in the morning. My sister and her family were already there. My good friends, Carroll and Penny, were also there for the day. The ramp to the U-Haul truck was at the same level as the first floor of the farmhouse, making it very convenient for loading. We worked all day, moving the really large furniture from the farmhouse to the new condo; it was tiring work.

My niece and nephew had warned me earlier that their father had a temper, and he wasn't in a good mood. Before leaving the condo, my brother-in-law came into the dining room table where I was seated with the others. Suddenly, he lashed out at me. "Now you think you're sitting pretty, huh?" he snapped. Other words followed, but I tuned all of them out, not saying a word.

When he left the room, my mother looked at me in total shock. She couldn't believe the way he had just treated me. My sister muttered that she was glad I didn't sass him; I should have asked her if she still wanted me as a sister! When I left my mother's condo that day, I returned to the farmhouse to work off some steam by thoroughly vacuuming all of the carpeted areas.

At Mom's funeral, Pastor Teitle said three words that I will always remember: "Martha had spunk." Yes, she definitely did! Pastor Teitle made me laugh at my own mother's funeral. He made me smile and remember her for the amazing woman she truly was.

Chapter 15:

Traveling Abroad

During my years at Bettendorf High School, I was able to travel outside of the United States during the summers. One trip was going back to Germany. But first, I decided to take a trip to Great Britain, and then I continued the journey to Norway. Only a bus tour can give one the feel for what London really has to offer: Tower of London, River Thames, Buckingham Palace, Westminster Abbey, St. Paul's Cathedral, etc. The performance of *Julius Caesar* at the Royal Shakespeare Theatre was tremendous. A member in a famous acting family was an actor in the performance. I toured Warwick Castle and Salisbury Castle, and dined on English-style breakfasts.

In Norway, I traveled from Bergen to Oslo with a group of tourists. I saw beautiful fjords in Norway; in winter, I'm sure it was the same. One couldn't help but to enjoy the picturesque scenery and unique attire of the citizens. Reaching Oslo, I boarded the passenger boat, *Kiel-Oslo-Kai*. However, it rained all day and all night so that I did not get to take in the scenic Baltic Sea, as my father had so often talked about. My cousin, Max Rühr, met me in Kiel. Naturally, old times began to roll again.

Max, his wife, Rosa, and my cousin Peter Artkämper's widow, Annelise, and I went to an operetta performance that was grand and glorious. We also went to the beach on the Baltic Sea and used the Strandkörpers again. Our conversations flowed like the sea; I realized how much I missed my family members. We were saddened by Klaus's passing; Max and Klaus had been brothers. But Aunt Emmy was still alive, even though she had a bout with breast cancer. In the province of Schleswig-Holstein, there was an outdoor museum showing styles of buildings from all different time periods.

We spent the whole day there. Upon departure, I could see the tears in Aunt Emmy's eyes. I gave her a big hug goodbye.

The second trip was to Australia and New Zealand. The National Education Association sponsored it. Our flight aboard a Boeing 747 landed in Honolulu, Hawaii, and continued on to the Fiji Islands. We had to disembark there because of an airline strike in Sydney, Australia. Around midnight, we arrived at our overnight accommodations only to find the pilots and stewardesses had gotten there first; there were no more rooms available! So, we got back in the car and journeyed over very bumpy roads some ten miles away to find new accommodations. I didn't get to sleep very well that night. My roommate snored the entire night.

When I got up around eight o'clock in the morning, I quickly got dressed and went to get breakfast. I went to take a sip of my tomato juice and noticed that a fly was swimming in it. *Disgusting!* I thought. There were screens in the windows, but there were holes in the screens. I shrugged it off; I wasn't going to let a little bug ruin the rest of my day while I was on vacation. Several of us rented a car so that we could tour the island. It was very picturesque! However, with storm clouds threatening everywhere, this didn't amount to much! At midnight the following night, we continued our journey to Sydney.

We made sure to tour the magnificent Opera House while we were in Sydney. That evening, several of us went to the Argyle Tavern for a full evening of entertainment. We had wisely made reservations. Most of the seating was on picnic benches; however, we were able to score a booth! After dinner, we spent the night listening to excellent live music. "Waltzing Matilda" was the first song that the band played. Then it just so happened to play all the songs that were popular when I was in high school. *What fantastic fun!* I thought.

The next day, we went to a sheep-shearing exhibition on a ranch. Our journey continued to Canberra, the national capitol, which was actually designed by an American architect. Melbourne was home to Captain Cook's cottage, and huge outdoor markets displayed piles of fresh fruits and vegetables all over the place. While I was in Melbourne, I met a husband-and-wife teacher combination. I learned from them that it was not uncommon to have seventy students in one classroom!

We flew to Alice Springs, which placed us in the outback. It was interesting to see the Aborigines; I hid my eyes behind my dark sunglasses. They had a nomadic existence and didn't wear shoes. On many nights, they slept in dried up riverbeds. Their eyes were so different than what I was used to seeing. Their eye sockets were sunk into their skulls. Later, we flew to Ayers Rock in a DC-3! Ayers Rock is a monolith of stone of great significance to those who had lived there so many years—the Aborigines. We then flew to Cairns on the Great Barrier Reef. What splendor we saw there! Cairns had a very tropical climate, and I wasn't going to complain about that.

We flew from Cairns to Sydney, with a short twenty-minute stop in Adelaide to meet my father's old friend, Hans Timm, and his family. Hans had emigrated to the United States and became a farmer friend of Dad's, while his sister emigrated to Australia. Our next stop was in Auckland, New Zealand—the land of multitudes of sheep. There is both a North Island and a South Island to New Zealand. The Southern Alps are on the South Island. This is where Sir Edmund Hillary was born and where he did his first mountain climbing. On the South Island, in the middle of summer, it still looked like the dead of winter. The Maoris—one of the six tribes of Polynesia—settled on the North Island. We noticed some volcanic activity in that area with mud pots and small geysers, too. Mostly, we saw sheep everywhere!

I brought a book with me from Iowa, the most thorough book I could find about the state. I gave the book to Jeanine Riessen Rennie's three sons. Jeanine and her siblings had grown up on a farm in Cleona Township in Scott County, Iowa, and Jeanine had arranged for me to visit a New Zealand elementary school. It was interesting to see the Maori children each wearing some form of red in their school uniforms. I had dinner at Jeanine and her husband's home. It was a lovely time. When the trip was over, it was time to head back to the United States. (Later, I learned of Jeanine's untimely death in an automobile crash. She was barely fifty years old.)

During another summer vacation, I figured it would be fun to take a trip to Alaska. I boarded the *ms Prinsendam* at Vancouver, British Columbia, to journey up the Inland Passage, gliding by Sitka with stops along the way at Ketchikan, Juneau, and Skagway. However, first we had to cross the Queen Charlotte Sound, about forty-five minutes in the open ocean. Admittedly, I became very seasick, and then some. Only apples and soda crackers helped bring me back to civilization.

Ketchikan school buses serve as tourist buses in the summertime. Ketchikan is known for its salmon canneries. The only way out of Ketchikan—unless one takes a cruise ship—is by airplane. Juneau, Alaska's capital, has parts that reminded me of the old Russian town that it once was. Sidewalks next to buildings had roofs at the first-story level because Juneau averages only fifty inches of rainfall each year. There are only fifty miles of roadway in Juneau, too. Skagway was an old mining town that was being converted into tourist items for sale. The railroad from Skagway took us to Whitehorse in the Northwest Territories. Once on the Alcan Highway, we traveled by bus to Fairbanks. During the night, it was a bit nerve-wracking to feel my bed shake—literally—from the earthquake tremors.

Denali embraced us with open arms. There was not a cloud in the sky surrounding Denali. Even when we reached our hotel room in Anchorage, Denali was still visible with no cloud cover at all. Our trip though Denali National Park was on school buses. We traveled over bumpy, rocky terrain that perhaps was only a trail, not a real road. My camera and telephoto lens could not be used on such a terrain. But, nevertheless, the wildlife was intriguing and exhilarating at the same time. Families of grizzly bears were in great abundance. *Denali, you beautiful Denali!* I thought as I took in the sights.

In Anchorage, we saw the Eklutna Indian Village and journeyed to Glacier Bay to see the ice blue Columbia Glacier. Later, Alaskan Airways took us to Nome on the Bering Sea. There, we saw the traditional Eskimo blanket toss. Whaling season was in full effect, and it was interesting to see the whalers do their work. Even with such long winters there, removing refuse is still a problem.

Caribbean cruises are always lots of fun in the sun. The *Jolly Roger*—a tourist pirate ship painted in tasteful red, white, and blue—took us from island to island on one day of the tour. The servers aboard the ship served a mighty good rum punch! Soon enough, the *Jolly Roger* dropped anchor before an island and let the tourists go to shore in houseboats to visit a concession stand. I decided to live a little. In my bathing suit attire, I jumped from a very heavy rope at the top of the ship into the Caribbean Sea. It occurred to me that I might never surface again, but eventually I did. Then I quickly swam to shore using the elementary backstroke.

After some time on the beach, the other tourists started to return back to the *Jolly Roger.* I swam back to the pirate ship, too, thinking, *Sharks!* A devilish grin spread across my face as I thought about what would happen if I really shouted out the word. After reaching the *Jolly Roger,* I climbed a rope ladder and then had to cross over a newly painted edge of the ship, slipping and sliding all the way. Was I a daredevil . . . or simply just a fool? Either way, it was an amazing experience.

Chapter 16:

Retirement

The principal at Bettendorf High School called me into his office to let me know that if I wanted to teach at Bettendorf High School the following year, I would be teaching Algebra 1A and Algebra 1B. In other words, he was stripping me of all the upper level mathematics courses I had. Yet, he had written a letter of recommendation for me for the 1995 Presidential Award for Excellence in the Teaching of Mathematics in Iowa. Sometime later, he lost his job as principal of the school because of illicit activities in which he was engaged.

On the last day of school, a luncheon was held in the high school cafeteria for all personnel working in the school district. The superintendent gave a brief biography of each person who was leaving. Accommodated alphabetically, I was the second to last person to be recognized. There were quite a few people who left that year. I wore my best dress and tried to look as natural as possible, being brave and trying hard not to shed any tears. When it was my turn to come forward, I took a step and suddenly everyone stood up. Shocked, I looked at them all as I received a standing ovation! No other teacher had been given one. I felt incredible, knowing that my peers held me in such a high regard. Apparently, this gesture was too much for the principal to handle; he quickly left the cafeteria.

I didn't know it at the time, but three of my stellar students from AP calculus got together the summer following my retirement and wrote a letter to the principal about the way he treated me. They expressed their displeasure with my untimely departure from the school. I didn't know this until I happened to run into one of these students in 2007 and he told me about it.

After reluctantly leaving Bettendorf High School, I accepted a part-time mathematics teaching position at a private school with a religious affiliation for three-and-a-half years. This school was just trying to get established, and it sometimes did not pay its teachers. I had made a sizeable donation to the school, so it deemed that other teachers should be paid before me. This made me angry and frustrated. The danger signals were out there, but I ignored them. The stress was absolutely horrendous, and I should have known better than to take this teaching position in the first place.

The school had few students with a wide range of abilities. I began teaching Algebra I, Geometry and Algebra II. I created a pre-algebra course when I realized that some of the students could not comprehend Algebra I. I had to add a general math class, too, for some of the other students who hardly understood the basics. With these students, I focused on developing good study habits. I did this with humor, hoping to obtain some kind of camaraderie. Both in school and after school, I monitored their study habits as they grew unexpectedly.

To illustrate this growth, one of those students later graduated and then began studying at a seminary, and two are now teaching at private religious schools: one in English and one in computer science. When I got to know my students better, they responded willfully. However, despite these successes, I was feeling the pressure of all of these teaching preparations along with the financial woes besetting the school. This pressure came to a head during the winter of my fourth year at the school.

In mid-January 2004, I was preparing semester exams on a computer at the public library. I let the time get away from me; the library announced that it would close in five minutes. I hurried to the main desk so that I could buy a disk in order to save my work, but the library employees had already shut the computers down. Frustrated and anxious, I went home and rewrote the exam by hand. Needless to say, I did not sleep well that night.

I overslept the next morning so I had to rush to work. While speeding in my car, I missed my turn from the interstate and made a U-turn on the divided highway in front of a semi truck, which had to cross part of the shoulder to avoid colliding with my car. An Iowa Highway Patrol officer who had been driving behind the truck promptly pulled me over in his cruiser. The patrolman would not let me drive my car because he thought I was delirious. And you know what? He was absolutely correct! This was a time that I was fortunate to have a police officer of the law stop me. I literally felt like I was slowly losing my mind. My bipolar disorder was acting up again.

I locked my car and left it on the right shoulder of Interstate-80. The patrolman then offered to take me to school. How many students have seen their teacher brought to school in an Iowa Highway Patrol cruiser? Nevertheless, I was immediately sent to the emergency room for a day of tests and then sent home. Dr. Sidecar got wind of the fact that I had been in the emergency room and asked to see me as soon as possible. He arranged for me to be hospitalized in a private room in the mental ward with no access to a corridor or a sidewalk outside. I was hospitalized there for about four weeks in an isolated room.

This was by far the worst bipolar episode I had experienced in my life. It was as if two individual bipolar episodes crashed into one another in my brain, causing my brain to function very poorly and my speech to become totally erratic. I felt like a zombie; I was completely out of it! When I was finally released, I still did not feel like myself. I was nervous, edgy, and couldn't sleep.

I was no longer able to finish my teaching assignment due to my unstable health. Dr. Sidecar took me completely off lithium because it was adversely affecting my kidneys. He tried many new medicines on me, but none of them seemed to produce the results we were looking for. Sleeping pills didn't help at all; in fact, they kept me awake. I was having the worst year of my life.

It took Dr. Sidecar a long time to find a combination of medicines that would work on me, helping me to function better, but he prevailed with the correct combination once again. As always, I was able to rely on my dear cousin,

Leland, and his wife, Lynn, to make trips to the hospital for me whenever I needed to go there. These days, Dr. Sidecar has me on a completely new set of medicines that are very effective. Through the whole ordeal, I never gave up because I knew there had to be a solution. Eventually, it presented itself.

Soon after I left the school, it filed for bankruptcy. I tried to get some of the donation I had originally given it back, but the school denied my request. I was amazed that none of the directors would recognize my donation so I could recoup at least some of it. I mean, the school didn't exist anymore! Unfortunately, my donation was gone and so was the school. I took comfort in the fact that the Lord knows what I had donated, despite the lack of recognition by the school's board of directors. The disappointment in the school did not help my recovery from my worst bipolar incident. I looked forward to better days, hoping they would soon come.

But they wouldn't come so fast. In January 2005, I was back in the hospital again. While there, I started bleeding from my uterus. Fibrous tissue had again filled my uterus from a previous D and C. Two pre-cancerous polyps were removed and sent by my gynecologist to university hospitals in Iowa City, Iowa. I was told that I should have a hysterectomy. And, wonder of all wonders, my kidneys began to function again! I was placed back on lithium carbonate. *Praise the Lord!* I thought. It was great to be feeling well again.

As I felt brave enough to open up to my family, friends, and colleagues about my bipolar disorder and the fact that I was writing a book about living with the condition, I received an array of different responses. However, I wasn't surprised by their reactions. People become uncomfortable when they are confronted with something they are unfamiliar with. Here is the list of reactions I received:

"Oh, oh! Oh, my. Oh, my. I didn't know . . ."

"I thought we hired a mathematics teacher?"

One woman said she knew of two people who had bipolar disorder and that they said they had difficulty sleeping. She listened intently to what I had to say and encouraged me to finish the book on my life.

One person simply got up from his chair and left.

One person was more enthusiastic than I was in writing this book.

One person agreed with the secrecy I had maintained while teaching at Bettendorf High School. He said the administration would certainly have taken me to task.

One person said, "Ugh, well, just plug along . . ."

One person asked lots of questions to make sure I was all right now.

One person just stared at me in utter silence.

What is your conclusion? Is it that some people have compassion and others don't? Is it that some people simply don't know what to say? All those years of secrecy should have remained a part of my life. It appears that the stigma of bipolar disorder is still part of today's scene.

Another incident of note occurred two weeks before Christmas in 2008. I was shopping in a local supermarket when a woman scurried toward me, shouting, "Miss Stuhr! Miss Stuhr!" She removed her sunglasses, and I still did not recognize her. She introduced herself as Caroline Holmsby. That's when I remembered she was an elementary school mathematics teacher in the Bettendorf school system. Her son, Jack, lived on the West Coast, but he always talked about me. Though it had been some ten years or more since he was a student of mine at Bettendorf High School, Caroline said Jack had always said that I was the best teacher he ever had at Bettendorf High School. I shook Caroline's hand and thanked her for telling me that.

In January 2009, I received a random letter from Mary Leahy, a former student of mine in 1976 and 1977 at Bettendorf High School. Excerpts from Mary's letter include:

> After I became a math tutor for my children's school, I started thinking of you often because I try to emulate your teaching style. I so appreciate your positive

influence in my life and wanted to write to thank you. I started at the University of Iowa in pre-nursing, and remembered you telling me that I should become a doctor, not a nurse.

You were the only one who took the time to encourage me to reach higher. You said I was smart enough. As it turned out, I took an anatomy course for nurses that required us to go to the cadaver lab with the med students. I asked one question that stumped the instructor, then took a minute and figured it out myself. That's when I remembered what you said about being smart enough and changed my major.

Now, all these years later, I am a gynecologist. I'm trying to instill in my own children and my math team at school the same love of math that you have. I remember the time you would take to tell us about everyday applications of what we were learning. It was an answer to the famous high school question: "Why do we have to learn this?"

You were always a good sport to answer the question with pertinent reasons. So I want to say thank you, thank you, thank you for being a shining light for me.

These are just a few examples of the wonderful testimonies I have had because I recognized and overcame my bipolar disorder.

In summary, my father was of high intelligence and had great courage. He recognized in me what had been in his family lineage. He helped me realize my condition and deal with it. After seeing his sister institutionalized and helping his brother, he knew I needed help and he kindly helped me. I was blessed with a loving father who went the extra mile to help me overcome my condition.

My mother was a perfectionist. She always helped others, had the patience of Job, and was full of wisdom. Furthermore, the woman had spunk and great powers of persuasion. She was much smarter than she thought she was. It was a true art form to watch her Americanize my father. She would never insult his intelligence; however, she'd just calmly line up alternatives for him to consider. The way she treated my father most certainly helped him with his short temper. I owe my success with dealing with my condition to my loving parents who never gave up on me. They proved that, through example, a healthy dose of patience, understanding, and courage can help anyone, including someone like me.

Lastly, Dr. Sidecar truly is a genius. He has me on medications that make me feel good about who I am. I can function normally in society without worrying about when my next episode will be. Throughout treatment, as my life circumstances change, and as I simply become older, my medications are monitored using blood tests to gauge my lithium and creatinine levels. Even though being diagnosed with bipolar disorder is serious, I have tried to lead my life with as much dignity, integrity, intelligence, courage, and strength that both the Lord and Dr. Sidecar have given me. I couldn't have gotten this far without either of them.

I wish the best of luck and great courage to everybody who has bipolar disorder!

Definitions and References

The American community, as a whole, does not understand bipolar disorder. It is viewed by society as a permanent condition rather than as one with a solution. Bipolar disorder is treatable—not curable—but recurrent in nature. The authors of the *Textbook of Psychiatry* have defined and clinically described "bipolar disorder" as follows:

Definition:

Bipolar disorder is genetic. According to the *Textbook of Psychiatry*, "Since the major effective illnesses, bipolar disorder and major depression, were derived from the concept of manic depressive illness twenty-five years ago, they have been found to be highly familial in a number of European and American families."

Clinical Description:

A diagnosis of bipolar disorder is made when a patient has a history of mania or hypomania. Key diagnostic of mania (see below) are a distinct period of elevated, expansive, or irritated mood accompanied by increased activity, pressure of speech, flight of ideas, grandiosity, decreased need for sleep, and/or distractibility. Some manic episodes are characterized by the predominance of euphoric-grandiose symptoms, while others show a dysphonic paranoid pattern.

According to the American Psychiatric Association, "manic syndrome" is defined as including criteria A, B, and C listed below; "hypomanic syndrome" is defined as including criteria A and B, but not C—no marked impairment.

- A. A distinct period of abnormally and persistently elevated, expansive, or irritable mood
- B. During the period of mood disturbance, at least three of the following symptoms have persisted (four if the

mood is only irritable and have been present to a significant degree).

   a. Inflated self-esteem or grandiosity
   b. Decreased need for sleep, e.g., feels rested after only three hours of sleep
   c. More talkative than usual or pressure to keep talking
   d. Flight of ideas or subjective experience that thoughts are racing
   e. Distractibility, e.g., attention too easily drawn to unimportant or irrelevant external stimuli
   f. Increase in goal-directed activity (socially, at work or school, or sexuality) or psychomotor agitation
   g. Excessive involvement in pleasurable activities that have a high potential for painful consequences, e.g., the person engages in unrestrained buying sprees, sexual indiscretions, or foolish business investments

C. Mood disturbance sufficiently severe to cause marked impairment in occupational functioning or unusual social activities or relationships with others, or to necessitate hospitalization to prevent harm to self or others
D. At no time during the illness have there been delusions or hallucinations for as long as two weeks in the absence of prominent mood symptoms (e.g., before the mood symptoms developed or after they have remitted).
E. Not superimposed on schizophrenia, schizophreniform disorder, delusional disorder, or psychotic disorder NOS